No Stray Bullets
The Making of an American Hero

Ruth Price
Mother of Daniel J. Price,
Marine Raider

© 2018 by Ruth Price
All rights reserved by the author, including
the right of reproduction in whole or in part, in any form

Contact the author at:
nostraybullets@gmail.com

- ENDORSEMENTS -

"Many will never know the courage and dedication shown by our men and women in uniform, especially those who made the ultimate sacrifice. 'No Stray Bullets' does a tremendous job of showing the heart, sharing the experience, and telling the story of Marine Gunnery Sgt. Daniel J. Price."

–United States Congressman Bill Huizenga

"Gunnery Sergeant Dan Price was a heroic warrior who had an unmatched work ethic and commitment to excellence. He epitomizes the words honor, courage and commitment. Dan Price will go down in the history of the Marine Raiders as a legendary warrior who refused to lose in combat. I had the honor and privilege to command Dan on two combat deployments and watch his heroic actions on multiple occasions. Not only is he one of the most gifted combat leaders in the history of the Marine Corps Forces Special Operations Command (MARSOC), he is one of the finest men I had the opportunity to know. This book is a fitting tribute to a Marine Raider that lived the life of 'Spiritus Invictus:' unconquerable spirit."

–LtCol Andrew Christian (Ret)
1st Marine Raider Battalion

"Dan was the quintessential operator and the best man I ever served with. I miss my friend, his foolish laugh, and his reassuring presence, every day. Ruth delivers a powerfully plaintive, yet pleasant account of this utterly selfless, valiant, meat eating, warrior-monk from the unique vantage point of an aggrieved mother. Ruth seamlessly leverages the temporal dimension to intertwine Dan's youth and adulthood—linking his career success factors, like leadership and combat prowess, to his formative childhood experiences, like trapping and animal husbandry. Dan's independence and iron will were clearly endowed at birth, cultivated during his upbringing, sharpened in Marine Reconnaissance, and attained perfect equilibrium as a MARSOC Raider. Prepare yourself for catharsis, with equal parts light-hearted joy and tearful sorrow at what the world lost when Dan's fire was extinguished."

– *Rob Younkins*
Marine Raider Teammate
MSOT 8111 1st Marine Raider Battalion

"*No Stray Bullets* is a story of a great American warrior told from the perspective of his mother. This story provides the background that depicts the deep commitment to raising a son the right way. It gives the reader an inside understanding of family life and shaping a boy into a warrior. Humor, love, education, and drive are themes of the story, provided by the family who lost a son in defense of this great nation."

–John
The Marine from West Michigan who Dan met in pre-BRC and escorted Dan's body home from Afghanistan

- CONTENTS -

Preface And Acknowledgments	6
Introduction	8
Glossary And Acronyms	10
1. The Final Mission	12
2. Childhood	15
3. Recruit Training	23
4. School Of Infantry, Pre-BRC, and BRC	34
5. First And Second Deployments To Iraq	43
Photographs	60
6. Marine Combatant Diver School, Wedding, And Scout Sniper School	70
7. Third Deployment And Leaving Recon Battalion	79
8. Shewan	90
9. Changes In Career And Personal Life	99
10. A Deployment Cut Short	105
11. Getting Back In The Fight	110
12. The End...And The Beginning	118
13. The Conclusion Of The Matter	131

- PREFACE AND ACKNOWLEDGMENTS -

For as long as I can remember, I have always dreamed of writing a book. This is not the book I would have chosen to write. I would have written an amusing account of raising children, living on a hobby farm, or owning pets. I may even have written about our son's career in the US Marine Corps. If so, I would have chosen a different ending. Instead, I have to write the story with God's ending. I have tried to be faithful in telling the story that God gave me.

Obviously, I was not a participant in all of the events that I tell about. I have tried to be as accurate as possible, but had to rely on my memory of what Dan told us. I was able to have Dan's military records sent to me from the Marine Corps Headquarters. Although much of that information was encoded, I was able to establish a timeline of promotions, deployments, and various schools Dan attended. General information gleaned from various internet websites was useful in adding context to specific events.

I am thankful for the relationships that we have been able to establish with former teammates and commanders from the 1st Raider Battalion. Those men loved Dan and have embraced us in the years since he was killed. They are our connection to the military and allow us to be a part of the close-knit brotherhood of the Marine Raiders. The military corrections given by these Raiders have served not only to improve the manuscript, but to enhance my understanding of how things work in the world of the US Marine Corps Forces Special Operations Community. As much as possible, I have attempted to protect the privacy and anonymity of any and all Marine Raiders referred to in this book.

For the past two-and-a-half years, this manuscript has been draining my emotions and energy. The support and encouragement of friends and family members has been invaluable in the completion of this project. I thank my family particularly for their patience in the last six months as I worked to perfect the manuscript and get it ready for publication.

Finally, I thank Greg Smith, my editor and literary consultant, for his efforts to instruct me on the fine points of writing, storytelling, and publishing. I may not have been his easiest client. Without his help, this book would not exist in its current form. It might never have reached publication. Greg pushed and prodded me out of my box of black and white chronological thinking and encouraged me to write the story with color and excitement. In working with him to complete this project, I have advanced my skills as a writer.

At his request, Dan's younger brother has been excluded from any photos, and I have minimized references to him in telling Dan's story.

- INTRODUCTION -

This story focuses on the life and death of a great warrior named Dan Price. The story provides plenty of detail about family life and military training. It is important to highlight, from someone outside of the family, the determination and strength the Price family has. I want to provide the reader with some information and examples the book does not cover. The Prices created an excellent home environment to raise their children and this environment along with a strong religious influence shaped their children into smart, capable adults. They nudged Dan in the right directions while he was growing up through homeschooling and good parenting. They provided an appropriate amount of guidance and direction after Dan departed for the Marine Corps which helped Dan make the right decisions in his military career. The Prices demonstrated a deep trust in God and incredible strength after Dan's death. I remember waiting with them at the church before the funeral started in a small room with some food and drinks. There was a piano in the room and after most of the other people in the room departed to get things set up for the funeral the Prices remained and started to sing hymns with Ruth playing the piano. The singing demonstrated to me their resolve and trust in God during a difficult time. It has stuck in my memory ever since. The resolve of the Prices during a very difficult time is impressive, and it is important to note the support the city of Holland and the Freedom Riders provided during this time. I escorted Dan from Afghanistan to Holland Michigan. I sat in the front seat of the hearse on the trip from the church to the cemetery. It is hard to put into words the experience of waiting for hundreds of freedom riders on motorcycles with American flags to depart the church parking lot to protect the procession. Once we got to the street, thousands of people lined both sides almost continuously from the church to the cemetery, waving flags and showing their support. It seemed as though the entire city of Holland stopped what they were doing to be present. It was an amazing experience that still moves me when I think about it six years later. No Stray Bullets is the story of the man who was shaped by incredible parents and an extremely supportive community.

–John

- GLOSSARY AND ACRONYMS -

Places and Terms:

Baghdis, Bagdhis, Badghis, and Badhgis: Multiple spellings and pronunciations of provinces, towns, and regions are common in both Iraq and Afghanistan. Therefore, all four of these spellings are acceptable and refer to the same location.

Billet: military job or work assignment.

Indoc: indoctrination or tryout exercises for acceptance into training schools for advanced military units.

Raider: name adopted by MARSOC in 2014 which carries on the legacy of the WWII Marine Corps Raider Regiment.

Recon: reconnaissance in general or more specifically Marine Corps Reconnaissance Battalions.

Acronyms:

ANA: *Afghanistan National Army*

ATL: *Assistant Team Leader*

BRC: *Basic Reconnaissance Course*

CACO: *Casualty Assistance Call Officer*

CWSS: *Combat Water Safety Swimmer course*

ESG: *Expeditionary Strike Group*

FOB: *Forward Operating Base*

HAHO: *High Altitude High Opening parachuting*

HALO: *High Altitude Low Opening parachuting*

IED: *Improvised Explosive Device*

ITB: *Infantry Training Battalion, one division of the School of Infantry*

MARSOC: *Marine Corps Forces Special Operations Command*

MCRDSD: *Marine Corps Recruit Depot San Diego*

MEU: *Marine Expeditionary Unit*

MMPC: *Multi-Mission Parachute Course*

MOS: *Marine Occupational Specialty*

MRE: *Meal Ready-to-Eat*

MSOT: *Marine Corps Forces Special Operations Team*

PFC: *Private First Class*

PFT: *Physical Fitness Test*

PT: *Physical Training*

PTSD: *Post Traumatic Stress Disorder*

PX: *Post Exchange, the military equivalent of a grocery or department store*

RPG: *Rocket Propelled Grenade*

SERE: *Survival, Evasion, Resistance, and Escape training*

SMTB: *Special Missions Training Battalion*

SOI: *School Of Infantry*

SOTF: *Special Operations Task Force*

- 1 -
THE FINAL MISSION

By eleven o'clock in the morning on July 29, 2012, the dust began to settle over the Baghdis compound, as the firefight came to an end. Two more shots rang out across the barren high desert within the Helmand River Valley. Then silence. The skirmish had been brief but violent—and deadly. Bodies littered the ground in and around the compound. The hot sun beat down on the carnage and seemed to intensify the silence. The bodies of several Afghan commandos and insurgents lay in the dust. Along with them lay the bodies of two US Marine Corps Forces Special Operations Command operators.

Dan's preparations for this mission began on July 28, 2012. After working a full day in the SOTF (Special Operations Task Force) office, he gathered and organized his combat gear. Dan hadn't used the gear since his previous deployment, a year ago. Now, he eagerly prepared to get back in the fight. After his preparations were complete, Dan tried to get a couple hours of sleep before showering. As he finished in the shower, his "friends" from the SOTF covered him with baby powder. He had been like a kid in a candy store in anticipation of the upcoming mission, and his co-workers took advantage of the opportunity to harass him. He good-naturedly headed back to the shower to rinse off before carefully putting on his combat armor and covering it with his camouflage uniform. In keeping with his character, Dan checked and rechecked his gear and provisions and headed for the landing zone to join Team 8232 for their early morning helicopter insertion. The final pre-dawn mission preparations were made, and the team settled into their hide site to wait for daylight.

As the sun rose hot and dry over the dusty earth, the Marine Corps Special Operations team waited for the Afghan commandos to take the lead in their attempt to take control of the compound. Shortly after nine a.m., the commandos launched the attack. The commandos crossed approximately 800 meters of scrub brush and desert gullies in order to reach the compound. The compound itself was surrounded by a two-meter high thick mud wall. It would have to be breached in order to gain entry.

It wasn't long before it became obvious to Team 8232 that the commandos were in trouble. Unexpected firepower erupted from inside the compound. Unknown to the team or commandos, a meeting of heavily armed top insurgent officials was being conducted at the compound. Several commandos were killed or wounded by machine gun fire. Dan immediately volunteered to accompany the team leader on ATVs to treat and move the wounded commandos from the battlefield to an area from which they could be safely medically evacuated.

It was somewhat ironic for Dan to be charging across 800 meters of rough ground under fire on an ATV. When he was twelve or thirteen years old, he had stubbornly persisted with incessant chatter to get permission to own a quad. When he finally purchased one, he spent hours riding quads and eventually dirt-bikes with his friends. On this particular ride, Dan charged into combat in an attempt to salvage a mission that seemed destined to fail.

The remaining commandos were pinned down. The mission was in jeopardy. The Marines were supposed to limit their involvement to training, supporting, and assisting the commandos. When things didn't go as planned, however, the team instinctively did what they were trained to do. They pushed the fight. The commandos didn't have the motivation or drive that the Special Operations Forces operators do. After assisting the wounded commandos, Dan and the team leader returned to the hide site to gather additional ammunition. Then they plunged across the open ground on the ATVs to assist the stranded commandos and finish the mission.

Taking careful aim, Dan was able to shoot an insurgent sniper, who was firing at the commandos from a window inside the compound. He and the team leader scaled the compound wall and climbed onto a roof. They began to drop grenades down chimneys and pushed the fight until it seemed that most, if not all, of the insurgents were killed. The two began a door-to-door search to finish securing the compound. The rough terrain and the wall surrounding the compound hampered the team's ability to see the progression of the firefight from their positions in the hide site and sniper overwatch. The two operators were on their own.

Suddenly, within the compound, the passageway between the mud wall and the building exploded in machine gun fire. One remaining insurgent had circled around behind the two highly-trained Special Operations Marines and opened fire on them. Their body armor absorbed many of the bullets, but the two operators had too much unprotected area. The machine gun at point-blank range peppered them with bullets. They were struck multiple times.

One bullet severed Dan's carotid artery. Both operators were killed.

After the shooting within the compound subsided, a sniper from Team 8232 was finally able to shoot the insurgent with two shots. The first took off his arm, the second killed him. Within less than two hours, the insurgent defense had been broken, and the compound was secured.

The victory came at a very high cost. The two US Marine Corps Forces Special Operations operators who now lay in the dust were described as the rock star Marine of the East Coast and the rock star Marine of the West Coast. They were the best of the best. The rock star Marine of the West Coast was Gunnery Sergeant Daniel J. Price.

Where do these heroes come from? We depend on them and assume that they will be there when needed. But that should make us ask hard questions. Are men like this born, or are they made? This is the story of Dan Price. I hope it helps you understand not only how he got from Holland, Michigan to the Helmand River Valley, but why.

- 2 -
CHILDHOOD

Dan's story began in the little town of Zeeland, on the western side of Michigan, about ten miles from Lake Michigan's eastern shoreline. Dan came into the world in his own stubborn and strong-willed way. The baby seemed very active throughout the pregnancy. Three days before my due date we went to a Ponderosa Steakhouse with friends and enjoyed a wonderful buffet dinner. When I stood up after dinner, my water broke. We hurried home and called the doctor. No labor developed overnight, but the next morning we went to the Zeeland Community Hospital so that it could be induced. Things progressed rather slowly throughout the day and evening, but finally around nine o'clock, the doctor said that I was ready. Nobody could know how unready we were to give birth to, much less raise, a child like Dan, but into the delivery room we went to welcome our first-born son.

After a lot of pushing and straining, the doctor finally asked for forceps. As the nurse rummaged for them and handed him a pair, the doctor said, "No, I need the long forceps." Oh boy, that didn't sound good. The doctor strained and pulled with his long forceps. We waited anxiously for a giraffe-necked baby to emerge with a flat head and horrible paddle marks on his face. At last, the doctor said, "One more push!"

Shortly before ten in the evening on June 8, 1985, Daniel Joseph Price was born. He weighed nine pounds, five and one-half ounces and didn't have a long neck or horrible forceps marks. He had a little tuft of soft dark hair on a head that was not flat at all. It was very round. He looked like a little old man, and we thought he was perfect. His forced entry into the world was the first of many battles fought before he reached adulthood.

Taking care of Baby Dan had its challenges. Dan was, as many infants are, quite impatient and demanding, but he was not a cuddler. He cried for attention, but then pushed away from any comforting. Many evening hours were spent hiking up and down the hallway in our tiny two bedroom mobile home, trying to console the crying baby. Dan had a voracious appetite that seemed never to be appeased. He ate cereal as soon as he came home from the hospital. The first couple of months were rough, but we made it through. After that, Dan settled and became a more contented child. He was very busy, so when he was able to move around and entertain himself a bit, he was somewhat easier.

When Dan began to toddle, we found out quite quickly that if he was busy, he was happy. This God-given personality trait grew along with him. Whenever we talk about Dan with guys he worked with or went to schools with, his work ethic is mentioned. The same is true of his determination and never-quit attitude. We worked hard to develop and shape Dan's strong will and not crush it. We knew that Dan would never get into trouble by being in the wrong crowd. Any trouble he got into would be because he chose to get into it. He would most likely be the leader of whatever crowd he was with. Although every child is special, Dan had the personality to lead and accomplish great things.

Dan had an active imagination and could play by himself very nicely. He also had a helpful nature. In a toddler, the combination of imagination, helpfulness, and the need for constant activity does not always culminate in pleasant results. One time when Dan's little brother was less than a year-old, I had to leave the two of them for a minute to move a load of laundry from the washer into the dryer. The baby was eating Cheerios in his high chair. I hurried from the laundry room to place a few more Cheerios on the tray and discovered that the newly-opened giant box of Cheerios was empty. The baby, the high chair, and much of the floor were covered with them. Dan was just trying to help.

Some of Dan's exploits didn't look even remotely like an attempt at helpfulness. One episode occurred while I was giving Dan's little brother a bath. Dan was awfully quiet in the other room, but I couldn't leave my infant son alone in the tub to check what his older brother was doing. I quickly finished the bath and took the baby into the bedroom. The dark blue carpet was now white, everything in the room was white. I could hardly see Dan, enveloped in a cloud of white, busily emptying the almost new, economy-sized baby powder bottle. If Dan wasn't kept busy with constructive activity, he made himself busy with his own fun and adventure.

Most of Dan's education was done at home, but he did attend Zeeland Christian Schools from kindergarten through second grade. Dan seemed to do well at Zeeland Christian, and we didn't discover until later that playground fights were not uncommon for him. Apparently, he knew the elementary school principal better than he should have. Dan claimed that the fights usually involved a playground bully who would not let the other children use the tire swing or some other playground equipment. Dan stepped in with his protective warrior persona and defended the rights of the weaker underdogs. This may have been the case, but it didn't justify fighting in my mind.

These playground fights may have been the catalyst for another situation that arose. Dan had never balked at going to school. Riding the bus had always been one of the best parts of his school day. Suddenly, he wanted me to bring him to school, or at least pick him up after school. After several days of telling him how ridiculous that was, the truth came out. A neighbor boy who rode the bus with Dan was looking for a fight. This boy was two years older and much bigger than Dan. Even though Dan did not want me to call Ross's mom, something had to be done. I called her. I don't know how things were "taken care of" at their house, but the next day Dan came home from school and told me that Ross had asked him to play cards on the bus on the way home. In the ensuing years, Ross and Dan became best friends and remained closer than many brothers until Dan was killed.

When Dan was a seven-year-old second grader, he came home from school one day and asked why our family was so different from everybody else's families. Dan had to ask for permission to watch TV, and TV viewing was closely monitored. His friends, one of them in particular, could watch what they wanted, when they wanted. While one of his friends seemed to be left on his own a lot, we insisted on knowing where Dan was and who he was playing with. We demanded that there would be parental supervision whenever he was at a friend's house. He was only seven. What would Dan be like in middle school if he displayed such an independent attitude in the second grade? Years later, he said that he would have ended up in the juvenile court system before he was fourteen years old if he had stayed in a regular school setting. I thank God for convicting us to begin homeschooling in Dan's third-grade year. By His gracious provision, we were able to channel much of Dan's excess energy into productivity.

Homeschooling may not work for every family, but it is probably the best child-rearing decision made by our family. I was able to make sure the kids were being diligent with their curriculum. They could go about their own activities as soon as the schoolwork and household chores were finished for the day. We had moved to a ten-acre hobby farm when Dan was three, and the opportunities for work and play there were endless. Our three kids spent a lot of time together exploring the barn and pretending to be pioneers and survivalists in the woods and by the creek. Much of their time was spent learning how to use tools and building things in the workshop. Our basement was full of John Deere toy farm equipment. Many hours were spent planting, cultivating, and harvesting crops. The boys engineered ways to make their farm work easier, and they built barns and sheds for their animals.

The kids usually had chores to help with before playing. When they were very young, I decided that if one of them did a job, I would not redo it to meet my standards. If the job was done to the best of the child's ability, it was a job well done. It didn't matter whether it was done well or not. We rotated jobs so all of the kids could learn how to do each job, none of us would get bored with what we were doing, and I would end up doing everything on a rotating basis. With this routine, it wasn't long before I realized that Dan performed most of the tasks just as well, if not better, than I did.

When Dan was eleven years old, he was asked to work on the neighbor's pig farm. The farm was owned by Ross's dad. This was the same Ross who had wanted to fight with Dan in the second grade. Now the two former enemies were not only friends, but worked side by side on the family farm. Dan's first job on the farm was to power wash the nursery rooms after the little pigs were moved out. It was not a difficult job, but it kept Dan busy and out of trouble.

Just a year later when Dan was twelve years old, the farm's full-time hired man slid off a barn roof while removing snow. He broke his right ankle and crushed his left heel. He was off work for months. When he returned to work he quickly realized that he was no longer able to be on his feet as much as the job required. He had to quit at the farm and find a different job.

Thinking the situation would be temporary when the hired man was first injured, Dan and Ross added his work to their own. Since Dan was homeschooled, he could work every afternoon. I began to assign his schoolwork so he finished a week of school in four days, leaving one day free to wash the nursery in the morning before beginning his afternoon work. At age twelve, Dan worked 30-35 hours per week on the pig farm, and kept up with seventh grade schoolwork. When it became apparent that the hired man would be unable to return to his job, Dan continued with his rigorous work and school schedule. He continued to add even more work hours until he left for recruit training.

Dan developed much independence and self-control by working on the pig farm. He began to show a rebellious streak mingled with just enough respect to avoid punishment. It was very frustrating to listen to his incessant arguing whenever he disagreed with our "unreasonable" parental decisions. When we explained our logic, he would get a certain shut-down look in his eyes that stated very plainly, "I hear you, but will not listen to you." He wouldn't vocalize that, but it was there to see. Once he enlisted in the Marine Corps, he told us outright, "I will obey now, but in July, I will be gone and won't have to listen to you anymore." I suspect the same shut-down look was presented to his drill instructors in recruit training.

While Dan was working on the farm, he decided that we needed a gas-powered power washer at our house. He researched it and talked about it for months before purchasing just what he thought we needed. When the power washer finally arrived, Dan proceeded to fire it up. It wouldn't start. Dan tinkered and fiddled. Eventually, he began to fuss and fume and get quite worked up. Fearing that he was going to break it before it even started, I timidly questioned whether there might be a gas supply that needed to be turned on. That is not what Dan wanted to hear from his non-mechanically inclined mother, so I quietly walked away to be busy elsewhere. After a while, I heard the motor catch and start, so I meandered back for a demonstration of how it worked. I casually asked if he had flooded it, or if he had discovered a problem. Dan just grinned a bit sheepishly and pointed to the little lever that turned the gas supply on and off.

• • •

I don't know exactly when Dan began to think about joining the military. His second-grade Sunday School teacher thought he would be a preacher. That involved way more schooling than Dan wanted to think about, and the job itself is full of books and studying. When Dan was five or six years old, we had a family friend who was in the army. He was deployed to Iraq in the Persian Gulf War and drove a tanker truck in a supply line. We befriended his young wife who lived just around the corner from us. Since we had a personal interest in the conflict, we closely followed all of the news reports of SCUD missiles, air strikes, and everything else involved with it. It is possible that Dan started thinking of a military career at that time.

When he got into middle school, we had many discussions about what direction his life would take. He enjoyed his work on the pig farm, and his boss really liked him. But it was a family farm, and Dan figured there was enough family involved. There would be no room for him on a long term basis. Dan began to take a special interest in current events and politics. He listened to a lot of talk radio, particularly Rush Limbaugh, while he was working in the barns and driving tractors on the farm. Since he was a great arguer and very smart academically, I suggested something requiring higher education, maybe law or politics. That, of course, involved more school than Dan was interested in. Not knowing what his specialty would be or where his calling would take him, I focused on building a foundation that would support him in whatever direction God would lead him.

Dan was a junior in high school on September 11, 2001. The kids were supposed to be working on their schoolwork in the family room while I was busy in the kitchen. As I worked, I overheard some chatter about the World Trade Center. I headed for the family room to redirect their attention to their schoolwork and realized that they had the radio on. When I told Dan's brother to turn it off and get busy, he told me that a plane had hit the World Trade Center, and another one had flown into it, too. I could tell that the boys were quite excited, so I decided to find out what was going on. After listening to the radio for a few minutes, we turned on the television and watched in horror as the fires continued to burn and both World Trade Center towers eventually collapsed. Life would never be the same for our nation, or our family, again.

The next several days were eerily silent. The nation was reeling, and each citizen was affected in some way. Our house is between Grand Rapids, Michigan and Chicago, Illinois. There are almost always jets and jet streams visible in the sky above. Air traffic was suspended following the devastation of the World Trade Center. Its absence was more obvious than its presence had ever been. The clear blue sky was completely void of the usual jet streams, and we noticed their absence. Dan listened to the news and commentary about all of it. He had a very strong sense of justice, and he knew that what had happened was not right. He was livid about a terrorist attack in our own country and against innocent civilians. Where is the honor in attacking unarmed civilians? What a cowardly way to do battle! He was determined to fight in an honorable way.

One year later, Dan enlisted in the United States Armed Forces. Ironically, the Marines were not his first consideration. He wanted to become a Navy SEAL. Dan researched and talked to recruiters from all the branches of the military and quickly dismissed the Army and Air Force. The Marine recruiter pointed out that if he didn't make it in the SEAL program, he could end up swabbing decks for four years in the Navy. The recruiter went on to say that every Marine is a rifleman first and foremost. The Marines are the first ground troops to be sent to any hotspot or conflict. That settled the matter for Dan. If he didn't make it into Recon or some sort of special operations, he would still get to fight. This decision was confirmed as he did more research. The Marine training is more rigorous than the other military branches, their warrior mentality is more evident, and their history is full of honor and combat. On September 20, 2002, Dan enlisted in the US Marine Corps Delayed Entry Program.

Dan was very busy in the ten months between his enlistment and the time he left for recruit training. In addition to keeping up with schoolwork and working on the pig farm, Dan began to prepare physically, mentally, and spiritually for the Marine Corps. He was an active member in the Holland, Michigan Marine recruit pool of prospective Marines. In the "pool," the "poolees" worked on PT (physical training), Marine Corps knowledge and history, and building brotherhood relationships. Dan's school curriculum was structured to prepare him for recruit training. He studied Marine Corps history, US Constitutional Law, and psychology based on what the Bible tells us about man's thoughts and troubles. Dan worked to develop habits that would help him trust in the Holy Spirit to strengthen him in God's Word. Military life would be quite different from our life on the farm. Here, Dan was fed spiritually as our family engaged in regular Bible reading, prayer, and discussions about what the Bible teaches. Several times during Dan's senior year, regular school curriculum was set aside so that we could discuss various questions, concerns, and issues that came up. Our time with Dan was short. It was much more important to talk through those things than anything that might be found in the books.

We were thankful for the mature young man that Dan had become, but we knew he was a work in progress. We prayed that God would guard his heart and protect his faith from attacks that we knew would come. At Dan's homeschool high school graduation ceremony, Karl encouraged him with words from the Bible that promise that God gives strength and prepares his people for battle. We trusted God to be with Dan and equip him for the task that was before him. We believed that God had claimed Dan as His own for eternity, had given him the "shield of salvation," and would guard and protect him. We were confident that God would enable Dan to subdue and destroy his enemies—physical and spiritual enemies.

Before leaving for recruit training, Dan sold his quad and put his truck for sale. He wanted to get rid of his stuff and live a simple life as a warrior. On Sunday, July 20, 2003, Dan left home to enter the Marine Corps Recruit Training Depot in San Diego.

– 3 –
RECRUIT TRAINING

After attending church and eating a simple lunch, we brought Dan to the recruiter's office in Holland. The recruiter drove Dan and two other recruits to the Military Entry Processing (MEP) Center in Lansing, Michigan. Dan was just a month past his eighteenth birthday. We had raised Dan for this step of independence, taking responsibility for himself, and being a productive member of society. Still, it was a very abrupt change for all of us. The separation during recruit training is a time of growth for the families as well as for the recruits themselves. Even though Dan was very busy at Marine Corps Recruit Depot San Diego (MCRDSD), he was painfully homesick during the thirteen weeks of training. We thought about him constantly and missed him in every daily activity.

Dan called once from Lansing, and we didn't hear from him again for more than two weeks. Although Dan was separated from us, the drill instructors exercised supreme authority and monitored the activity of the recruits very closely. The recruits had almost no free time and very little opportunity to get into serious trouble.

Dan's first letter home from recruit training was a form letter. It was written in his penmanship, but the words came right out of the Marine Corps Handbook. The next letter we received was more personal and sounded like Dan had actually composed it himself. From then on, the letters trudged slowly back and forth across the country via snail mail. It was frustrating on both ends. By the time I could respond to something that Dan had written about, he was far beyond it in his fast-paced training schedule. He desperately wanted to hear about the routine daily activities at home, and I encouraged him with words of scripture in the daily letters I sent him. I did not trust the drill instructors with his moral and spiritual growth.

Dan had worked hard while at home to enter recruit training in excellent physical condition. One of Dan's drill instructors told us that Dan was the most physically fit recruit he had seen. In his last year at home, instead of riding his quad to work, Dan had run the half mile through the cornfield in his work boots, so he would be prepared to run in combat boots. He bought a membership at the community aquatic center to improve his swimming techniques and skills. In order to perform the required number of pullups to get a perfect score on Physical Fitness Tests, Dan had hung a pullup bar in our garage. Each morning before starting school, Dan drank a glass or two of water. It wouldn't be long before he needed a bathroom break. Then he did as many pullups as he could, drank more water, and went back to his schoolwork. Eventually, he would have to pee again, and the cycle repeated itself. Although twenty was the required number of pullups for a perfect score, Dan was soon doing thirty pullups on a regular basis. On the Initial Strength Test upon entering recruit training, Dan came in first in the mile-and-a-half run. He even beat the drill instructors with his time of eight minutes. He did the required one hundred crunches and twenty pullups for a perfect score of 300.

Before leaving for recruit training, Dan was a leader in the Delayed Entry Program recruit pool. The recruiter had depended on him to work with and encourage some of the less motivated poolees. In recruit training, he continued to be given leadership opportunities. He was the platoon guide on and off throughout training. He found out later that he didn't learn the drill steps quick enough to satisfy the senior drill instructor. It is not surprising that he didn't excel in drill exercises since he entered the Marines to be a warrior, not to march straight and look pretty.

Dan was given the responsibility of teaching some of the other recruits various knowledge items from the Marine Corps Handbook. It was encouraging to be able to put his study of Marine Corps history and regulations to good use. Dan also became a spiritual leader in his platoon. He was appointed to be a "lay leader" who helped the chaplain in preparing for Sunday worship services. During the actual worship services, Dan helped to pass the bread and juice for the Protestant communion services. As lay leader, he enjoyed being allowed to attend an extra Bible study during the week. Since Sunday was the one day that was a little bit different than the others, the recruits measured their remaining time in training by how many Sundays were left. Everyone went to church. Dan was noticed and respected by the other recruits because of his physical fitness and leadership qualities. This gave him the opportunity to talk to the other recruits and explain his reasons for maintaining moral purity and protecting virginity. In little ways, he was impacting the lives of his fellow Marine recruits.

Dan did well with the discipline and structure of the Marine Corps. When he was very young, he and his siblings turned an old granary on our property into a workshop. Dan had a place for all of his tools and possessions, and everything was always in its place. In training, the games of the drill instructors annoyed him, but didn't throw him off course. The drill instructors liked to come into the barracks in the middle of the night and dump the contents of everyone's foot locker into one huge pile on the floor. It didn't take Dan long to find his things and get squared away again. Some of the recruits, on occasion, lost their cover (hat). They would then be required to hold their hand over their head as a makeshift cover whenever they were outdoors. They were shamed until they had an opportunity to purchase a new cover at the PX. Dan never understood how they could lose a cover. He always had an extra one to loan out to someone who had lost theirs. Later when Dan lived in an apartment or a house, he had many totes of gear in his garage. From time to time various teammates wanted to borrow something from him. They could call him while he was out in town, or even gone on deployments, and he could tell them exactly where to find the tote that contained whatever they wished to borrow.

Dan had somewhat of a love/hate attitude toward recruit training. He did have some fun, but at the same time, he could hardly wait for it to be done. Training was, according to Dan, "like prison with no end in sight." He stressed over every test and qualification that he encountered. While he looked forward to the swim qualification, he felt bad for the many recruits who couldn't swim. Dan was anxious about his PFT scores and the high confidence course. He was afraid of heights and didn't know how he would react to the obstacles before him. Drill tests continued to challenge Dan. He asked for prayers in all of these matters.

Everyone gets sick in recruit training. They work hard and don't get a lot of sleep. If the recruit gets sent to "medical" it is very possible for him to get placed in a different platoon with a later graduation date. When Dan got sick, he welcomed the immunization and antibiotic injections. One night, he woke up and scraped pus from his tonsils with a large wooden Q-tip used to clean rifles. When the cotton end didn't scrape it clean, he used the wooden end. After that episode, he wrote in one of his letters, "My tonsil that at one time filled half my throat with its white ugly self, is starting to recede." He was willing to do whatever it took to stay on track. He did not want to get sent to medical or be delayed for any reason.

In recruit training, Dan was surrounded by chaotic circumstances. He desperately wanted to graduate from recruit training with a promotion from private to private first class. He was learning to maintain order and equanimity in his own life. He just needed to focus on the job at hand in order to achieve his goals. It was a lesson that he continued to hone throughout his Marine Corps career. Dan wanted to excel at every challenge that he encountered, not just get through them.

The recruits were allowed to receive almost nothing from home. Any sort of care packages, cookies, and personal items were forbidden. Each letter they received had to be paid for with push-ups. After a few weeks, the recruits were allowed to receive power bars. Dan got plenty to eat, but thought that getting power bars would be "kind of cool," so we sent them. The recruits were supposed to eat them in a certain area with no sharing. Typical of Dan, though, he broke a piece off from his power bar and threw it to one of his friends. He was just a little disobedient, but not really bad.

Near the end of recruit training, Dan received a package from a very proper older lady in our church. From the contents of the package and the accompanying letter, it was clear that she was completely clueless about the Marine Corps recruit training program. The package contained rifle magazine loaders that her company made. In the letter that came with it, the lady inquired as to whether Dan attended the United Reformed Church in Escondido. Marine recruits in training have no vehicle, no free time, and no liberty to come and go. The recruit training depot is located almost forty-five minutes from that particular church.

The letter went on to tell Dan that she "would tell you about the pretty girls [in Dan's home church], but I don't know which ones you are interested in…by the time you're twenty-five they'll look pretty good." Then she explained about the magazine loaders: "I'm sending you a magazine loader for your rifle for target shooting. If you don't load your own magazine, give it to the sergeant or whoever is in charge of loading the rifles. See how they like it. We make them, and think they're pretty good!"

One can only imagine the reaction of Dan's drill instructors as the package was opened, the contents revealed, and the accompanying letter read. With expletives deleted, it went something like this:

DI (red-faced and screaming): "Price, who sent this package to you?"

Dan (shouting at the top of his lungs, as is proper for recruits addressing superiors): "Sir, a lady from this recruit's church, Sir!"

DI (incredulously): "What kind of a church do you go to, anyway?"

Dan never did see the magazine loader again after this encounter. Apparently, it went to the "sergeant or whoever is in charge of loading the rifles."

A month into recruit training, Dan scored another perfect 300 score on a PFT. He had done twenty pullups, 104 crunches, and had run three miles in a time of 17:40. He was the second recruit out of almost 600 in the company to complete the run. He was awarded a phone call home for his efforts. We were at our county fair, so he called his maternal grandparents. We received a full report of his ten-minute call. Dan sounded fine, although his voice was a bit raspy. We assumed that was from being sick and having to yell everything all of the time. We were thankful to have heard from Dan, even if it was second-hand.

The second phase of recruit training was done at Camp Pendleton. After only one meal there, Dan wrote that the food "was good, but not as good as MCRD. You also don't get as much." That's about as much as Dan ever said about his accommodations anywhere. He was so focused on doing the job at hand that he didn't notice weather conditions or quality of food or accommodations at any of his training locations or on deployments. If asked, he usually had to look outside to see what the weather was like. He rarely complained, but one time asked for seasoned salt to be sent to him. Apparently, the MRE's (Meals Ready to Eat) they were eating in Iraq all tasted the same.

Upon arriving at Camp Pendleton, the recruits were issued field gear. They were required to carry their gear in packs wherever they went. The recruits spent a lot of time in the field, hiking and training. Whenever they were away from base, they ate MRE's, which Dan liked. He enjoyed the difficult hikes and embraced the challenge of hiking with a heavy pack.

The recruits also received rifle training during second phase. After a week of shooting classes, they were finally allowed to shoot real guns. Dan was reminded of the "good times at home." He was nervous about the rifle qualification and again wanted not only to qualify but to excel. On the day of qualification, Dan shot 227 out of a possible 250. He met his goal and qualified as an expert in marksmanship. He was excited that he could, "Reach out and touch someone at 500 yards. Hoo Ra!!!" (The correct expression is actually, "Oorah." A Marine would never say "Hoo Ra." Dan, either in recruit ignorance, or making a spelling error, wrote "Hoo Ra" in his letter home.)

Although Dan wanted to be either the platoon guide or a squad leader, he was not put in that position. Instead of sulking or feeling sorry for himself, Dan used the time those positions would have required for extra studying and working on his physical strength. He wanted to come out of training in better shape than he went in. He worked hard and had fun doing it.

On "bad days" when there wasn't much training scheduled, the drill instructors played mind games with the recruits. That made Dan angry. He wasn't afraid of hard work, but he hated senseless busyness. Dan wanted to be productive. He didn't enjoy stupidity for someone else's pleasure or because some of the recruits were not measuring up to what they should be. During those times, Dan wore the closed look that screamed, "I'll do it, but I won't be submissive about it." Dan was looking forward to doing more worthwhile activities. An eight-mile ruck hike and the Crucible loomed on the horizon.

Dan was allowed to call home a second time. It lasted only five minutes, but boosted his morale to talk to someone at home. Shortly after that phone call, Dan began what is supposed to be the hardest two weeks of recruit training. The first was field week. The second contained the Crucible.

He missed some daytime infiltration classes on the first day of field week because of interviews regarding a Presidential Guard billet. Dan had been selected for screening for this position earlier in training before coming to Camp Pendleton. At first, he had the option whether to be considered for this or not. He wasn't sure he would like the job and he asked for input from home. Presidential Guard is a three year billet, either at Camp David or in Washington D.C. It involves a lot of close quarter combat training and consists mostly of formal guard duty. It is a prestigious position, but does not include combat and would prohibit Dan from trying to get into Recon for at least three years. Although Dan was honored to be considered, he was relieved when the screeners at Camp Pendleton figured that he was a better warrior candidate than Presidential Guard candidate and dropped him from the selection process.

Dan enjoyed the rest of the "most difficult" two weeks of recruit training. He loved the gas chamber training, and even though he didn't require a breath when they had to take off their gas masks, he took one, because he, "Wanted to know what it was like. It was pretty strong." Dan always wanted to live life to the fullest and experience everything he could along the way. The rest of field week was, as one would expect, spent in the field eating MRE's and doing a lot of hiking. The recruits engaged in substantial amounts of daytime and nighttime shooting. Dan had loved shooting guns at home. Now he was able to do it in preparation for his life's occupation. The highlight for Dan during field week was when the drill instructor handed him a full rifle magazine and told him to empty it as fast as he could.

The Crucible receives a lot of hype, and probably because of all the talk about it, Dan expected it to be more difficult than it was. The Crucible is the culmination of the recruit training program. It is a fifty-four hour exercise that tests the endurance and abilities of each recruit. Working on teams, the recruits engage in problem solving exercises, land navigation courses, and obstacle courses. During the fifty-four-hour Crucible, the recruits march over forty-five miles carrying fifty pound ruck packs. They are given only two or three MREs to carry them through, and they get only about six hours of sleep. The final Crucible element at Camp Pendleton is the climbing of "The Reaper." The Reaper is a mountain with steep inclines that must be conquered. Upon reaching the summit of The Reaper, the recruits are awarded the Eagle, Globe, and Anchor pin and congratulated as "Marine" for the first time. Following the completion of the Crucible, the recruits are treated to what is known as the Warrior's Breakfast. For the first time since arriving at recruit training, they are allowed to eat as much as they like of foods that have been denied them for 10 weeks. Although Dan claimed that the Crucible wasn't as bad as he anticipated, he did acknowledge that The Reaper "kicked his butt."

Following the completion of the Crucible, the recruits headed back to MCRDSD for the final two weeks of recruit training. Being third phase recruits gave them superiority over the newer recruits on base and put them closer to graduation and ten days of boot leave. Dan was looking forward to being home, doing things with friends, and having one of Mom's burgers. He had two weeks of testing and qualifications to get through before that. He passed his final swim qualification with a "First Class Alpha," which is good, but not quite first class. Dan still hoped for a promotion to PFC, possibly as a reward for his physical fitness test scores. His drill instructor informed him that he was close to having the highest PFT scores in the company. Two weeks before graduation, Dan was required to turn in his Alpha jacket to get PFC chevrons put on. The promotion seemed more probable, but Dan wasn't assuming anything. He was hoping for a perfect 300 score on his final PFT.

Typical of military planning, Dan was scheduled for oral surgery to remove a couple of wisdom teeth the day before the final PFT. He was on "bedrest" the day of surgery and "light duty" the day after. The day of light duty conflicted with completing the PFT with the rest of the company, so Dan had to do it one day late. He did his required number of pullups and crunches for a perfect score. All that remained was the three-mile run. He ran valiantly, just two days after having his wisdom teeth pulled. Toward the end of the run, Dan passed a group of new recruits. He had bloody froth drooling down his chin as he staggered toward the finish. The new recruits gazed in awe and wondered what they had signed up for. Dan finished the run with a fast enough time to earn a perfect score on his final PFT in recruit training. Even though he had the highest cumulative PFT in the company, the award and recognition went to another recruit. Dan's final score came in a day late. Dan's senior drill instructor was upset about the lack of recognition, but Dan didn't care. He got his promotion to PFC and had the satisfaction of knowing that he had achieved the highest PFT score in his company. All of the other recruits in the company knew it, as well.

The day before recruit training graduation, the families of the recruits were allowed to watch the recruits practice drill maneuvers on the parade deck. Each family member along the parade deck tried to identify their son or brother. Almost 600 recruits were all dressed the same, had identical haircuts, and were trained to walk and maneuver in exactly the same manner. We finally spotted Dan. Then, from the subdued, almost fearful crowd, my dad yelled out, "Hey, Price!" Dan's smirk confirmed that we were watching the recruit that would be coming home with us.

After drill practice was completed, Dan was called into the drill instructor's office to explain. The unauthorized smirk in response to Grandpa's greeting now had to be accounted for. When asked who had yelled to him, Dan responded, "Sir, that was this recruit's grandfather, Sir!" The drill instructor simply stated that he had better be glad it was his grandfather.

Dan was relieved that there were no repercussions and no penalties to be paid. The recruits did their final motivational run that morning. As they ran in formation, each platoon shouted cadence in response to the prompting of their platoon guide. Finally, the recruits dressed in their uniforms and assembled for the Eagle, Globe, and Anchor ceremony. After that came the time we had all been waiting for. The recruits were granted "on base liberty" with their families.

Dan spent the next six hours with our family: dad, mom, two siblings, and three grandparents. He showed us where he had lived for the last twelve weeks. Dan showed us the high confidence course and took us to the PX. We accompanied him to get a haircut and were able to observe his new table manners. It was amusing to watch him pick up a glass in the same way a toddler does and hold it with both hands. When we gave him a hard time about it, he said he wasn't taking any chances on being held back at this point. He would do whatever it took to assure his departure from MCRDSD. He had a way of doing whatever foolishness was required and maintain a level of pride in doing so. Dan returned to his barracks thirty minutes early that evening. He wished to avoid any possibility of causing trouble in this final stage of recruit training.

Graduation exercises were finished by noon the next day, and Dan was released with his meager possessions to spend the next ten days on leave. He was not the same young man who had left us three months earlier, and yet, he was. We had ten days to explore who he had become and how our relationships had changed.

That evening, Dan took out the iron in the hotel room and began to iron and detail his uniform. It was obvious that the Marine Corps was only going to encourage some of Dan's quirks and obsessions. The neatness factor was exaggerated, if that was even possible. When Dan was a toddler, he had gone around the house pointing at every fuzz he saw on the carpet. "Ucky, Mummy, ucky, ucky," he said. It was kind of cute in the beginning, and I humored him by picking up the fuzzes that he pointed out. After a while, though, it was annoying, and I told him to pick them up himself. He did just that, until we got him a toy vacuum cleaner for a gift. It seemed the perfect solution, except that it didn't really work. He went over and over and over every fuzz. When his vacuum cleaner didn't pick up the fuzzes, he became frustrated. Eventually, I allowed him to use the regular vacuum and let him vacuum to his heart's content. Upon graduation from recruit training, Dan became one of the most squared-away enlisted Marines the Corps had ever seen.

Dan greatly enjoyed his time with friends and family during his boot leave. He hung out with friends, visited restaurants, worked out with the local recruit pool, and looked forward to returning to Camp Pendleton for further training. One day, he and a group of friends and family went to Silver Lake State Park for quad and truck riding in the sand dunes. On that day, Dan demonstrated his quick thinking reactionary skills. He had left his dirt bike at home. He did not want to take any chances of injuring himself by doing something reckless or stupid. He spent the day riding with others in various trucks. He was, of course, the center of activity and the life of the party all day long. Suddenly, out in the dunes, one of the truck engines started on fire. Dan quickly jumped out of the vehicle he was in, ran to the truck on fire, and got everyone out. He then popped open the hood and started to throw sand on the engine. In just a few minutes, the fire was out. The truck was towed to the parking lot, and after an hour or two of "wrenching," was good to go back in the dunes. The rest of the day was uneventful, and Dan was the hero of the outing for his quick action.

In spite of Dan's growing independence and knowledge, he sometimes demonstrated a lack of maturity and judgment. One afternoon, he showed his two siblings and me a fast-moving motivational DVD. The DVD had heavy metal music accompanying rapidly changing scenes of Marine training exercises. Dan seemed to have forgotten that we were not Marine recruits in need of physical and emotional motivation to get the job done. We were his mom and siblings "down on the farm" in Michigan. I was hoping for some commentary from Dan to explain what was happening in the video, but conversation was impossible with the volume level where he deemed it necessary for the proper effect. I left the room in a state of emotional collapse.

My reaction resulted from a combination of events. Three months of missing Dan during recruit training had taken a toll. We had just returned from our trip to California, and I was recovering from its stress. The immediate circumstance with the DVD put me over the edge. After only a few minutes, Dan came to find me and apologize. I explained my fears for him, for who the Marine Corps wanted to make him, and for the ungodly environment and leadership that he would endure. He tried to assure me that he was who he was, and that no leadership would change his faith in Christ.

I didn't argue with him, but I had a greater appreciation and knowledge of how Satan works to undermine God's control in our lives than what Dan did at that time. I comforted myself with the assurances from Scripture that all things are under God's dominion. "Nothing can separate us from His love." "No one can snatch His sheep from His hand." God is good. He uses every circumstance in our lives to teach us and to draw us closer to Himself.

On the day before Dan had to fly back to California, he took a Sunday afternoon nap. I called gently from the bottom of the stairs a couple of times to wake him for a light supper before the evening worship service. Although he answered, he didn't get up. Apparently, he was not really awake. Dan had told us how the drill instructors woke the recruits every morning during recruit training. One of the drill instructors came quietly into the barracks and, with no warning, flipped on the lights and yelled, "LIGHTS, LIGHTS, LIGHTS!" The recruits were required to jump out of their racks and stand at attention immediately, if not sooner. Armed with this knowledge, I went upstairs to Dan's room. Quietly, but firmly, in a conversational tone, I said, "Lights, lights, lights." He was up and standing at attention beside his bed in his underwear so quickly that it scared us both. He looked at me, groaned rather sheepishly, and sat back down on the bed. In between giggles, I explained that I had called a couple of times. When he didn't get up, I came upstairs to wake him. After I had my humor under control, I apologized and told him I wouldn't do it again.

Dan was definitely growing in independence and capability as a confident Marine. He considered the "place where he lay his head at night" to be "home." Our house, although still home, was a place to rest and enjoy family time. Any other place Dan found himself was a place to experience whatever there was to experience in that place. It didn't matter whether it was in a barracks, out in the field, or in a tent on deployment somewhere. Our relationship with Dan had changed and was changing. We all had some adjusting and figuring out to do. Dan's Marine Corps career would be an adventure for him, but we would all be participants in it.

- 4 -
SCHOOL OF INFANTRY, PRE-BRC, AND BRC

Dan returned to California after his ten-day "boot leave" eager to further his training. After recruit training, Marines enter the School of Infantry (SOI), where their training is directed in one of two directions. Marine Combat Training (MCT) is a basic combat training course designed for new Marines that will have a military occupation other than infantry. These occupations may include cook, truck driver, administrative position, mechanic, or other occupation. Dan intended to become a warrior, so he was sent to the Infantry Training Battalion (ITB), which teaches the new basically trained Marines how to operate in combat in a warrior unit. The aspiring infantry members took courses in combat, land navigation, and weapons. Once again, hiking was a frequent activity and was done with full gear and packs. The new Marines also engaged in a lot of PT, or physical training.

Dan's homeschooling background had prepared him well for the training he was now receiving. The attention to grammar had helped his reading comprehension skills, and he easily understood the things he was studying. It also helped in writing various reports. We had been able to identify areas in which Dan was weak and spend time to strengthen those weaknesses. Dan had wished he were in a regular high school, so he could just fail and not have to rework his algebra problems. He often had to redo 50–60 percent of them because of careless mistakes. Now, particularly with regard to land navigation, he wished that he had applied himself more diligently to his math, algebra, and geometry studies. Although he hadn't learned all there is to learn in high school, he had been given the tools to learn. He had the ability to achieve whatever goals he would establish in his career.

An unofficial homeschool course that proved helpful to Dan in this more advanced combat training was wrestling with his brother. It had consumed a large chunk of Dan's middle-school class time. Often when they were supposed to be working on their schoolwork, a lot of bumping, thumping, and grunting sounds would come from the schoolroom. At those times, I went to check on their progress and found a tangled mass of arms and legs in a struggling mess on the schoolroom floor. I was incredulous as to how Dan could get his schoolwork done in time to go to work every afternoon. Aside from the algebra, he seemed to manage it, and excel.

One morning at ITB, while it was still dark, Dan and a few other students were roused from their racks and taken to the pool. There, they were told to climb a ladder to a small platform thirty feet above them. From that vantage point, the pool below could not be seen in the darkness. The students were instructed to jump into the unseen pool below. This was Dan's introduction to a mandatory indoc (indoctrination) screening for Recon training. Since that had been Dan's primary goal in joining the Marines, he was ecstatic that he had been chosen. Although the screening process was very demanding, Dan endured it and became eligible to enter the Basic Reconnaissance Course (BRC).

Dan completed his training at ITB in December of 2003 and began pre-BRC in January of 2004. This course is designed to condition Marines for BRC. Dan moved into the Recon squad bay and began a new normal. Recruit training and ITB had been quite easy for Dan compared to the training he received in pre-BRC. He wasn't sure he could make it. We assured him that he just had to take one day at a time, do his best at whatever the day brought, and leave the results up to God. Dan was finally being pushed hard enough to discover what he was capable of accomplishing and how to reach the limits of his potential.

Dan had always been apprehensive about new things. When he first worked on the pig farm at age eleven, he spent weeks of angst about his job. That job was to power wash the nursery rooms that had been emptied of pigs. It was not a difficult job. His boss showed him how to do it and left him alone to figure out the details. For months, on the night before he had to go to work each week, Dan lay awake in distress. On occasion, he even cried. He was afraid of failing. He wanted to do a good job, but was unfamiliar with the equipment, the work, and the farm. He was only eleven years old, but he would not quit. Eventually he learned to do the work quickly and efficiently. He was able to stop worrying about removing every last speck of pig poop on each slat and crate. It was an excellent opportunity for a young boy to develop character traits that would prove to be priceless for a Recon Marine, who had to think on his own and get the job done.

With each new challenge that Dan encountered, he worried that he would fail and disappoint us, his recruiter, or his instructors. He was never afraid of the training or anything associated with it, other than the possibility of failure. Because of this, Dan would never quit at anything. While he was in pre-BRC, one of the instructors recommended that he enroll in the Combat Water Safety Swimmer (CWSS) course. Dan found out later that the instructor wanted him to fail at something. With a failure rate of over 65 percent, he figured CWSS might be the thing. CWSS is a very grueling two-week course designed to teach Marines how to save people in the water without getting drowned themselves. One of the students that dropped out of Dan's particular class had tried out for a US Olympic swim team. Obviously, he was an excellent swimmer. Although Dan enjoyed the water and could swim alright, he had never had extensive swim instruction and was not an expert at all. The only advantage he had in CWSS was the fact that he would not quit.

Every day in CWSS began with swimming 500 meters and continued with other "fun" water exercises. The students were required to tread water wearing cammies with bricks in their pockets. Sometimes, they would have to tread water holding bricks above their heads. Almost every student needed to be rescued from the pool at one time or another. Dan slowly sank to the bottom of the pool one day while treading water, and stayed there. One of the instructors finally went in and motioned to him to drop the bricks. Dan was dragged out of the pool, given oxygen to help him recover, and sent back into the pool for more. During one qualifying underwater swim, Dan became disoriented and swam a very circuitous route. Although he covered way more than the required distance, he never reached the finish point. With almost no rest, Dan was sent back into the pool and instructed to try again, but to, "Swim straight." This time he completed the qualifying swim.

A quote from H.E. Jansen describes Dan's perseverance: "The man who wins may have been counted out many times, but he didn't hear the referee." Dan wasn't always conventional in his successes, but he never quit, and that made all the difference between success and failure.

While Dan was at pre-BRC, he met John. Since John was a corporal, and Dan a lowly PFC, the meeting was a little awkward at first, at least for Dan. Fraternization between ranks was just not to be done. But John was from Michigan, and one day while they were tying knots, Dan said something about Michigan. John asked him where he was from in Michigan, and they soon discovered that their families' homes were about thirty minutes from each other. John had gone to a Christian school and had a very similar background to Dan's. The two went to CWSS together and in the following years, attended many other schools together. They pushed each other to excellence. Their friendship lasted until John escorted Dan's body back from Afghanistan 8½ years later. When the guys first met in pre-BRC, they told their parents about each other. The parents, too, were able to establish an enduring friendship.

Dan and John both made it through pre-BRC, which boasted a failure rate of 80 percent. They proceeded on to BRC. BRC was a brutal, thirteen-week course of PT, land navigation, and various other amphibious training exercises. Although the training was rigorous, Dan had fun. One day, while practicing to call in artillery support, Dan decided to call in using the name "Big Richard" instead of his assigned call name. He made it through about half of a sentence before he was interrupted and reprimanded to, "Be serious and quit goofing around." He was fully capable of goofing around and still get the job done, as he had shown when wrestling with his brother during home school hours.

One of the amphibious exercises that the BRC students engaged in was making "sugar cookies." The students ran along the beach for miles in full gear with packs. After a while, they were instructed to drop their packs and enter the ocean. When the swim was completed, the students came out on the beach and were told to make sugar cookies. They were to roll around in the sand until they were completely covered inside and outside of their cammies. The fresh sugar cookies would gather their packs and run several more miles along the ocean, now chafing with wet sand inside their uniforms.

One of the swimming exercises in BRC was called "bobbing." In spite of Dan's success at CWSS, this was a very difficult and unpleasant pool exercise for him. In the bobbing exercise, the students were supposed to blow as much air out of their lungs as possible and sink to the bottom of the deep pool. Dan was naturally quite buoyant and had to work really hard to get to the bottom of the pool. When the students got to the bottom of the pool, they were supposed to push off with their feet, go back to the surface, grab a quick breath, and repeat the exercise immediately. One day while the BRC students were bobbing, one of the instructors motioned to John to stop and wait a moment. Dan exploded out of the water at the top of his bob. With a sound that was half-growl and half-moan, he grabbed his quick breath before descending again. The instructors and John had a good laugh at Dan's expense. Dan always admonished everyone else, with no respect to rank, to, "Suffer in silence," whenever they complained. Although Dan rarely complained about anything, the groaning during bobbing was a reminder of when Dan had the stomach flu in his mid-teens. He lay on the sofa and moaned for several hours before he finally vomited. He was really sick, but it was as pathetically funny as his groaning during the bobbing exercises.

While training in BRC, the guys enjoyed weekend visits to the Olive Garden restaurant. Because of the intensity of the training, they could hardly get enough calories to sustain themselves. Since Olive Garden offered unlimited salad and breadsticks, the guys went in, ordered their meals, and ate for hours. As long as the salad and breadsticks continued to appear on the table, the waitresses were well-compensated. Dan had always had a voracious appetite, and with his enormous physical activity, he couldn't get enough to eat.

One time, after consuming his complete meal along with an ample amount of salad and breadsticks, Dan ordered an entire cheesecake. He and his friends were able to eat half of it. The remainder was taken back to the barracks and enjoyed later.

On Sundays, Dan and John usually attended Escondido United Reformed Church. After the morning worship service, they were almost always invited to someone's house for dinner. They felt bad about eating so much food, but they burned so many calories during the week's training activities that they were constantly hungry. One of those families shared a memory with us after Dan's death. As the meal came to an end one Sunday, Dan politely inquired as to whether one of the children was finished with their plate. He was assured that the child was finished. Accompanied by giggles from the children, Dan took the plate and ate the scraps of fat that remained on it. Nothing would be wasted!

The intense physical demands of becoming a Recon Marine exceeded anything that Dan had experienced previously. And yet, he discovered that he had more to give. One day on a ruck hike, the BRC students came to the bottom of a hill. One of the students set down his pack and planned to quit. He could not continue. Rather than leaving him at the bottom of the hill,

Dan picked up the seventy-plus pound ruck that belonged to the exhausted student, tossed it onto his own seventy-plus pound ruck, and started up the hill with close to 150 pounds of gear on his back. After Dan was killed, this Marine, who had advanced to the Raider Battalion, introduced himself to us and told us about the incident that occurred in BRC. We remembered that Dan had told us about it. The young man said that without Dan's help on that day, he would not have passed BRC and become a Recon Marine, much less a Raider. He is one of the many men sprinkled throughout Dan's Marine Corps career who have been hugely impacted by Dan' s work ethic, strength, character, and sense of humor.

Dan and John both completed BRC and graduated on June 3, 2004, in a class of forty-four young men. They both followed these unofficial rules for Recon Marines:

1. *Always look cool*
2. *Never get lost*
3. *When in violation of rule 2, follow rule 1*

That very accurately describes Dan's calm and in-control demeanor. He was excited to be a part of this elite group of warriors. He could hardly wait to get integrated into one of the teams and get on with his career. While struggling through pre-BRC and BRC, Dan had questioned whether he had made the right choice in going to BRC immediately after ITB. Many of the guys he had gone to recruit training with were already deploying to Iraq. His doubts would soon be alleviated. He had a few more things to learn and a few more schools to attend, but soon, he would be ready to deploy with the Recon Battalion.

• • •

Every Recon Marine must receive SERE training. SERE is an acronym for Survival, Evasion, Resistance, and Escape. There are several SERE schools within the military which are located in various places around the country. Each SERE school, based on its location and environment, specializes in a different type of survival. Each school is tough and presents mental and physical challenges for its students. Dan went through the two-week SERE training at the naval base on Coronado Island. It was exactly what Dan loved to do and what he had enlisted in the Marine Corps for. All of the pioneer and survival games that Dan had played with his siblings while growing up on the farm were now reenacted on a much more serious level.

In the survival training portion of the course, the students learned about wilderness survival. They were taught what plants, insects, and animals are edible and which contain the most nutrition. After the classroom instruction was completed, the students were sent out to survive in the wilderness for several days. Dan was sent out with a survival team of about twelve guys led by a female Navy lieutenant. The lieutenant had recently graduated and had no previous field training or experience. It didn't take her long to see Dan's leadership capabilities, as well as his knowledge of the field. She informed him that when they had to do land navigation, he would be in charge. Dan had received extensive land navigation training in pre-BRC and BRC. It is interesting to note that before joining the Marine Corps, he rarely knew where he was. It had always been a challenge for him to find his way to any destination. Now, he led a group of military personnel including a higher ranking officer.

Dan had done a lot of reading and studying about wilderness survival in middle school and high school. He had also done a lot of muskrat and raccoon trapping. His expertise in these areas paid off big time now. In their quest for survival, Dan's team came upon a turkey nest containing about a dozen eggs. Most of the team was pretty excited about the prospect of boiling the eggs and having a nourishing meal. Dan loved adventure and challenge and told the team, "We can eat eggs now, or we can wait and have turkey for dinner and eggs for breakfast." That sounded great to the rest of the team, so Dan set a snare and waited patiently, knowing that the hen would come back to her nest.

That evening, Dan's team ate roast turkey, while the other teams survived on geckos. The following morning, Dan's team ate boiled eggs in various stages of development. One of the eggs had an advanced embryo inside of it. Nobody wanted that one when Dan offered it. One of the guys asked him if he was really that hungry. In reply, Dan popped the whole thing in his mouth and munched happily away on it. It was good protein, and he would not waste it.

The turkey that Dan snared is the only one in SERE school history to be caught. The director of the school went out to the field and had a picture taken of the team with the turkey. The picture hung at the school until it was given to us in 2015. Several years after Dan completed his SERE training, his wife flew alone to California after a visit to Michigan. The man in the seat next to her found out that her husband was a Recon Marine, and he began to tell her about a Marine he had heard about that snared a turkey in SERE school. The man told her it was the only turkey to ever be caught at SERE school. She calmly stated that she knew all about that story, because her husband was the Marine that had set the snare and caught the turkey. We were all proud of Dan's accomplishments.

The next element in SERE training was evasion. The students worked in two-man teams. Dan and his partner were the last ones to be "captured." Dan did such a good job of evading capture, that the instructors finally had to make him surrender.

In the resistance phase, the students are taught to resist enemy interrogations in captivity. At first, Dan wouldn't play the game. He said that he was, "Dead in like, less than five minutes, but then they made me play the game the way they taught us." The goal of resistance is to give just enough information to be kept alive, but not to give any information of real value. Dan assured us that we didn't have to worry about him lasting long as a POW. He would fight to the death before being captured. If he would be captured, he would play no games. He planned to antagonize his captors until they killed him. This was probably true. It was not a comforting thought.

After completing SERE training, Dan moved on to Assault Climb School in Bridgeport, California, near Yosemite National Park. Dan enjoyed this five-week course learning how to use ropes, crampons, anchors, and other climbing gear. Dan particularly enjoyed going out in the wilderness and practicing his new skills. He took beautiful pictures that showed how much he loved rock and mountain climbing. During one weekend off, several of the guys went on an extended mountain hike. After hiking for several hours, they found a suitable location for some cliff jumping into a lake far below. They camped in the open, then did some more swimming, diving, and hiking before returning to their barracks. Dan laughingly stated that they had been careful about diving into water of unknown depth from high cliffs.

At lunch time one day, the Assault Climb students discovered that adorable chipmunks had found their sack lunches and helped themselves. This was not to be tolerated. Dan devised a plan to protect the lunches. He used a skill similar to one that had been used at a campground years before, when several ducks made a nuisance of themselves around our family campsite. Dan, along with his dad and brother, set up a box with a stick attached to a string. They placed bait underneath the box. When the ducks went in for a snack, the string was pulled, leaving the duck trapped inside the box. The trappers and the observers were kept occupied for a long time with this activity. The ducks were eventually released to make a nuisance of themselves once again. The chipmunks did not have such a happy ending. For them, Dan found a large flat rock to prop up with a stick. Tasty morsels from lunch were placed under the rock. When the unsuspecting chipmunks went to enjoy them, the string attached to the stick was pulled, and the rock fell. "Voila! Got another one!" After ten or fifteen of the chipmunks were placed on a neat pile, one of the instructors caught on to what was happening and put a stop to it. One of the students who had heard stories of Dan's trapping days wondered if he could skin one of the chipmunks. In short order, Dan peeled the skin off the little chipmunk, stretched the pelt out to dry, and presented it to the guy.

In the fall of 2004, shortly after graduating as the Honor Graduate from Assault Climb School, Dan headed for jump school in Fort Benning, Georgia. This was Dan's least favorite training school. He was somewhat afraid of heights, and this three-week course taught the students the art of becoming what Dan called "glorified lawn darts." The jumps at this school were conducted with a static line that automatically opened the parachute as the student left the airplane. If the student didn't jump out of the plane correctly, the wind tumbled them along and into the side of the plane. The landings for static jumps tended to be rather rough. Each time Dan did a static jump, he worried about injuring the ankle that he had sprained in Assault Climb School. Several years passed before Dan was able to attend freefall school. In the meantime, in order to retain the monthly jump pay, he had to requalify periodically with static jumps. Dan never conquered his fear of heights, but he learned to channel his fear, in many circumstances, into productive energy and activity.

- 5 -
FIRST AND SECOND DEPLOYMENTS TO IRAQ

After over a year of training and attending schools, Dan was ready to prepare for his first deployment. He hadn't been back to Michigan since boot leave. John hadn't been home for a while either, so the two decided to come home together for a Thanksgiving weekend pre-deployment leave. We were eager to see Dan and meet John. We looked forward to spending some time with the boys and John's parents while they were home. While we waited with John's parents for the plane to land in Grand Rapids, Dan and John were impatiently waiting in the circling airplane. The plane circled for over an hour above a blanket of thick fog that hovered over the ground. When it became obvious that the plane would not be able to land that evening, it was redirected to Detroit, hours away from home. Dan and John were told that they would be booked on the first available flight to Grand Rapids the following morning. This was not an acceptable solution for the new Recon Marines, so they took matters into their own hands. Although neither was old enough to rent a vehicle on their own, Dan reported, "With John's diplomatic skills and my brute strength, we were able to convince the rental agency to give us a vehicle." Dan and John arrived at our house almost five hours later. After a breakfast of pancakes and eggs, John left in his rental vehicle and we were left to visit with Dan.

For the next five days he filled our home with his whirlwind presence. Dan participated in extended family Thanksgiving celebrations. We were thankful for that since his upcoming deployment would have him far away over Christmas. On the day after Thanksgiving, Dan had plans to meet John at the YMCA near John's house for some necessary working out. It's what Recon Marines do, even on days off. Dan loved working out. He figured it was his job, he got paid to do it, and someday staying fit would probably keep him alive.

How Dan excelled like he did in his career is somewhat surprising. Around home, it seemed as though he didn't always think too clearly. Getting to the YMCA that day was one of those times. He hopped into the newly acquired family minivan and punched the button for the garage door opener. As he put the vehicle into reverse to back out of the garage, the backup beeper was sounding. Not knowing what the noise was, and not bothering to find out, Dan began to back out of the garage. I was in the barn doing chores and heard a sickening, scraping sound. I exited the barn to see what had made the noise and observed Dan sheepishly examining the bruised back side of my minivan. The garage door had stopped its ascent and remained about a foot short of fully opening. Dan had backed into it with the upper portion of the back end of the vehicle. After getting the door open, he continued on his way to find John at the YMCA. To complete the story, Dan, with all of his land navigation skills in the Marine Corps could not follow the simple directions he had been given to find the Y in town. He had to call John who gave him step-by-step instructions as he found his way.

The next night, our family met John and his parents at a climbing-wall facility. Dan and John had done some climbing together in California, and Dan was certainly eager to show off some of the skills he had learned in Assault Climb school. We had an enjoyable time climbing under the watchful eye of the instructor at the facility. We listened politely to his instruction even though the two Marines with us knew more than he did. We had a great time getting better acquainted with John and his parents and deepening our friendships with them.

● ● ●

Upon his return to California, Dan eagerly engaged in pre-deployment workups with the same energy that he had begun his trapping business when he was twelve or thirteen. He had gone to trappers' conventions and talked to trappers who had been trapping for years. He gleaned whatever information he could. Then he bought traps, lure, pelt stretchers, skinning and fleshing knives, hip boots, shoulder-length rubber gloves, and all sorts of other equipment. He learned to make black walnut dye to soak the new traps in and dyed his hands in the process, too. Dan wasn't too concerned about counting up the cost of his trapping endeavors any more than he counted the cost now in his Marine Corps adventures. He immersed himself in learning and preparing to the best of his ability.

Because of his recent acceptance into the Recon community, and because he had attended so many schools since finishing BRC, Dan had missed most of the team preparations for this deployment. Now, he participated in at-sea periods for weeks at a time and engaged in various training exercises. He received extensive first aid training which included emergency wound treatment, insertion of IV's, and basic trauma care. Because a corpsman might not be available to help the wounded, each Recon Marine had to be able to start an IV. They practiced on each other and inserted IVs in all extremities. With combat injuries, it was likely that legs and arms might be missing.

Each team member was required to have a basic knowledge of every other team member's job. Any one of them could be lost on any given mission. Those remaining would have to cover for those missing. The team members were given a personal gear list as well as a team gear list of items to gather and pack in preparation for the deployment. Dan enjoyed the packing and preparing, planning and training as much as he had enjoyed camping preparations when he was young and pretended to live off the land at state parks. He took along extensive gear back then and was a master at packing a ton of stuff in limited space. He always knew where each item was. The skills that had been honed in play would now be used to preserve life.

Dan was quite concerned about being accepted by his Recon team. He was not only new to the Recon Battalion, but he was new to the Marine Corps. Dan was a "boot," brand new with no experience. Most of the team had previously deployed together and had some combat experience. In an effort to get to know the team and gain acceptance, Dan spent most of his off-duty hours with various team members. Since many of them lived in the barracks and had no family around, they soon became each other's family.

Dan was only nineteen and not allowed to legally drink alcohol. By default, he was often a designated driver. On one outing, a group of Marines went out in two vehicles. They parked both vehicles and all went inside of a bar. When they came out later, both vehicles were gone. Apparently, they had been parked illegally and were towed away. The guys stood around wondering what had happened to the cars and how they would get them back. Dan wandered around a corner and spotted one of the vehicles. The towing company had moved one vehicle around the corner and towed the other away. They planned to come back for this one. Before they made it back, however, the Marines came out of the bar, Dan found the vehicle, and drove up with his laughing face hanging out of the window. It wasn't long before he was fully accepted as a valuable member of the team. He took charge, made things happen, and made every place he was a happier place to be.

As eager as Dan was to engage in a deployment, he was a bit disappointed with his first one. He deployed with the 15th Marine Expeditionary Unit (MEU) on December 6, 2004. The MEU was part of Expeditionary Strike Group (ESG) 5 which deployed on a "routine Western Pacific deployment in support of the global war on terrorism and other missions as assigned by naval leadership." In civilian language, the ESG was to be a presence in the Western Pacific and Indian Oceans. Its general objective was to guard Iraqi oil terminals and conduct maritime security. It would also be available to do whatever it was called upon to do. The ESG included several vessels: the command amphibious assault ship USS Bonhomme Richard, amphibious ships USS Duluth and USS Rushmore, guided-missile cruiser USS Bunker Hill, guided-missile destroyer USS Milius, and frigate USS Thach. ESG-5 carried approximately 5,000 military personnel and was able to carry out almost any combat or humanitarian aid related mission. Because of the company of Recon Marines attached to it, ESG-5 was deemed Special Operations Capable (SOC). This term is unique to the US Marine Corps and means that ESG-5 was able to conduct non-conventional operations in addition to conventional operations.

Even though the ESG wasn't primarily a combat unit, Dan hoped that the MEU, or at least the Recon attachment with it, would get "in country," meaning Iraq, for at least a brief time before the deployment was finished. In the meantime, he was quite bored with life on board ship. Dan was assigned to the ship's laundry room. His co-worker there was a female sailor, with whom he did not get along very well. He found her to be arrogant, inefficient, and unprofessional. Dan was always thankful for the fact that women were not allowed to be part of the Marine Recon Battalion. He did not believe women belonged in the military. He worked with them if necessary and treated them with the respect they deserved as women and fellow service members, but he avoided interacting with them whenever possible. Dan did not enjoy his time on board ship.

After a week at sea, ESG-5 arrived in Pearl Harbor, Hawaii. The Recon Marines had three days of liberty to explore the island. Dan was excited to be seeing some of the world. He enjoyed hiking and snorkeling on and around Hawaii. The Marines were required to participate in a Marine Air Ground Task Force (MAGTF) run, which doesn't sound like much fun. Even though Dan didn't enjoy running, it was still exciting to be part of an impressive, mile-long line of Marines running in formation, chanting cadence, and proudly displaying their colors.

On December 26, ESG-5 left Hawaii and headed toward Guam, where they planned to spend several days for the New Year's holiday. Before they could reach Guam, a 9.0 magnitude earthquake struck the northern area of the Indonesian island of Sumatra. The resulting tsunami devastated ten island nations in the South China Sea. The expected five-day port stop in Guam was condensed to several hours, just long enough to refuel and take on aid supplies.

ESG-5 was sent immediately to provide humanitarian aid to the areas affected by the tsunami. They remained in the area for almost three weeks and provided medical help, engineering and construction help, and water purification equipment. In addition, they conducted search and rescue operations and ferried needed supplies to the islands. Dan didn't get off the ship during this time. He was kept busy packing skids of food, bottled water, and other disaster relief supplies to be transported to shore. He was too far offshore to see anything of the devastation on land but saw a lot of debris floating in the water surrounding the ship. Dan thought that some of the debris looked like bodies of animals or humans, but he couldn't be sure of it.

Over a million pounds of humanitarian relief supplies were sent ashore during Operation Unified Assistance. Dan, along with the other military personnel involved, received Humanitarian Aid Ribbons for their part in the relief efforts. Dan was promoted to corporal while engaged in the humanitarian efforts near Indonesia. While he appreciated the promotion, he was more excited about the prospect of leaving the area and heading towards the Persian Gulf in anticipation of getting into Iraq.

On January 26, 2005, the ESG arrived in the Persian Gulf. The Marines and their gear disembarked into Kuwait for combat training and instruction in the techniques used in the Central Command Area of Operations in Iraq. 1st Recon Battalion's Charlie Company, the company that Dan was part of, finally reached a Forward Operating Base (FOB) near Baghdad, Iraq on February 15, 2005. They engaged in what the Marine Corps calls security and stabilization operations within the northern area of Babil province.

Babil is a desert area with daytime high temperatures averaging 55–60 degrees Fahrenheit and nighttime lows averaging 40–45 degrees during the months of February and March. The dust is annoying, and dust storms are common. Dan hardly noticed the uncomfortable conditions. He was so excited to finally operate as a Recon Marine in a combat zone. When the nights became too cold to be comfortable, Dan buddied up and slept double with a friend in his sleeping bag.

Dan was his team's radio operator. He handled himself in a highly-professional manner with no goofing around as he had done while in BRC. The patrols Dan engaged in on this first deployment were mostly uneventful. His team encountered very little enemy opposition. During one operation, Dan was responsible for sending radio communications to give another Marine company information about a safe landing zone. His flawless communication of key information to surveillance and reconnaissance centers about helicopter landing zones in his team's area of operation were recognized as enabling the safe insertion of the entire company. After the completion of the deployment, Dan was awarded a commendation for his "outstanding tactical and technical proficiency as both a communicator and an operator."

On April 5, after only two months in country, the Marines from 1st Recon Battalion, Charlie Company, headed back to Kuwait. They packed their gear and boarded the USS Bonhomme Richard for the voyage back to California. Dan looked forward to experiencing more of the world on the way home. The USS Bonhomme Richard visited Brisbane, Australia on May 10-15, 2005. Dan had not yet attained the rank of sergeant and was required to return to the ship each night. During the daytime, however, he explored as much of Australia as he could reach. He was able to do some snorkeling among the scenic reefs off the coast. Dan did some other sightseeing, and he shopped for souvenirs for the family. He sent an ornately-decorated boomerang to us, and a koala bear necklace to his sister. Both souvenirs were greatly appreciated, not because of their beauty or value, but because they were sent by Dan. They indicated that he thought about family while he was on the other side of the world.

After the MEU left Australia, Dan struggled with boredom and trying to keep himself busy until they returned to California. He spent time in the ship's gym and internet café. They were very busy during the daytime, so he often visited those facilities at night. He didn't waste a lot of time on the internet, but he worked out and ran on the treadmills in the gym.

Dan wasn't much of a sailor, and there were times on the ocean when the ship rolled and lurched. Sometimes, it was hard to stay on a treadmill. One time when he was running, the ship made an unexpected dip, and suddenly the treadmill was no longer underneath him. Dan rolled across the gym floor, gathered what little pride he had left, and headed back to his rack. The sailors, who were more used to the lurching and rolling of the ship, gazed at him in amusement and continued with their workouts. Whenever the sea was calm enough, Dan ran in the open air on the flight deck. He was very happy on June 6, 2005, when the USS Bonhomme Richard returned to Pier 8 on Naval Station San Diego. The deployment hadn't been the exciting combat-filled deployment that Dan had anticipated, but it was a beginning. Dan saw some of the world, gained experience, and learned a great deal from his fellow Marines.

• • •

When Dan left for recruit training, he had resolved to live a simple warrior's life with no "stuff" to hold him back. After he returned from his first deployment, the desire to have his own transportation became stronger than that resolution. Many Marines return home from deployments and spend a lot of money on large purchases. Deployments offer an opportunity for service members to make a lot of tax-free money. Combat bases are located far from home. There are very few things to purchase on deployment bases other than small items for immediate use. Having been deprived of the material wealth they are used to in Southern California, Marines often come home ready to buy really nice, expensive vehicles and other toys.

Dan succumbed to his desire for transportation and bought a motorcycle. He didn't make a hasty decision. He thought about what he really wanted, what would best fulfill his needs, and what he would have fun with. He would like to have a nice, fancy truck but didn't want to spend the money. Because Dan lived in the barracks, he had to plan for storing a vehicle when he deployed again. Dan missed riding his dirt bike, it hardly ever rained in California, and he could store a motorcycle in a buddy's garage for nothing when he deployed. After all of the options had been weighed and considered, the decision was made. Dan purchased an affordable "crotch rocket."

Dan didn't have the bike for long before he crashed it. He was riding with a buddy who had his own bike. They were enjoying the California summer in bumper-to-bumper traffic in downtown Oceanside. Dan accelerated and scooted to squeeze between two vehicles as he merged into an adjoining lane. He checked his blind spot. As he did so, the vehicle in front of him in the lane he was entering hit the brakes. Dan didn't see the brake lights in time. He scooted too fast and hit the stopped vehicle. Down he went. Dan proved to be much more durable than the bike. He was uninjured. The bike was in a repair shop for the next several weeks. Once again, Dan was without transportation and had to depend on others to get where he was going.

The motorcycle stayed in the shop until shortly before Dan deployed again. He had somehow wiggled his way from Charlie Company to Bravo Company which was in the midst of workups in preparation for a September deployment. Although he would be joining a new team again, it wouldn't be as hard this time. Dan's team leader from his first deployment was also transferring to Bravo Company. Dan would be joining that team. Although Dan was behind again in workups and deployment preparation, his reputation as an operator was being established. Many of the guys knew him.

While Dan was growing and maturing professionally, he was struggling spiritually. His strong religious upbringing seemed to get in the way of hanging out with the team and being accepted by them. He tried to live like they did and still remain true to his faith. Although Dan set certain limits to his behavior, he began to compromise his conservative principles. Drinking became routine, and Dan made several weekend visits to Tijuana, Mexico, with various team members. Nothing good happened in Tijuana. TJ, as the Recon Marines fondly referred to it, was a place of filth, excess alcohol consumption, prostitution, and very crooked law enforcement. Dan soon figured out that he couldn't afford to get too drunk in Mexico, because, as he stated, "Someone had to stay sober enough to get us out of trouble and safely back to the barracks." Since Dan was a bit of a "control freak," he took it upon himself to control the circumstances and at least make an effort at taking care of his teammates.

Dan was open and honest about his activities. From the time he was very young, he had never been interested in lying about his behavior. He did what he wanted to and saw no need to cover it up. Being Dan's mother gave me license to counsel and parent him in spite of his age and independence. He listened respectfully, and did what he wanted. I hoped that, in time, God would convict him of his foolishness and reform his behavior.

Before he left for the Marine Corps, Dan had attended a high school prom with a girl from the group he hung around with. She was a junior in the local Christian high school and was looking for someone to take her to the junior-senior prom. Dan wouldn't listen to any arguments about the wisdom or foolishness of this idea. He believed he could just date her a few times and walk away to join the Marines. Although he tried to do that, the walking away didn't work out so well for Dan. On Labor Day weekend of 2005 that girl flew to California to visit Dan before his upcoming deployment. They planned to attend the wedding of one of Dan's teammates.

Dan's top priority at this time was his team, not the girlfriend's visit. While Dan joined his Marine buddies for the bachelor party, his girlfriend joined the group of unfamiliar girls for a bachelorette party. Many details of the outings are unknown, but assuredly, alcohol and some less-than-decent activities were involved in each of them. Several of the guys were riding in a rented limo when Dan decided that the moon roof should be opened. He unlocked the latch and pushed up on the moonroof. The entire thing flew off the top of the vehicle and landed on the I-5 freeway behind them. It is anybody's guess as to what carnage took place behind them. The Marines all shared in the expense for the damaged moonroof and thought it made a great bachelor party story.

The remainder of the weekend was comprised of more events that were far from keeping with Dan's upbringing. In spite of that, when his girlfriend flew back to Michigan, she and Dan were engaged. While Dan was gone on his second deployment, she would plan their wedding. It would take place the following summer when he returned home.

A week after Dan's girlfriend left California and returned to Michigan, Dan endured what became known as "The Madres Visit." Dan's friend, John, had also found a spot in Bravo Company and was planning to deploy in September. John's mother and I flew to California to visit the two before they deployed. The boys had instructed us to call them when we arrived in California, so that we could make arrangements to meet them. We received no answers to our attempted phone calls and decided to find our way to the 1st Recon Battalion barracks on our own.

We meandered through Camp Pendleton in our rental vehicle. Camp Pendleton is huge. We drove through some business areas and then into what appeared to be a wilderness. The terrain is rough, rocky, and somewhat mountainous. Periodically, we saw signs designating certain ranges or training areas. The sky was clear, the sun shone brightly, and it was pleasantly warm. We loved exploring the environment our sons called "home." John's mom had been to Camp Pendleton before and some of street names and areas were familiar to her.

We finally found the 1st Recon Battalion barracks and began to make inquiries as to where our sons might be. After a few minutes of a yelling relay game that involved several young Recon Marines, we heard a burst of uncontrolled laughter. Then a voice hollered, "Price's mom is here? I didn't think Price had a mom!" After several more minutes of uncomfortable waiting, Dan and John finally came out to greet us. Dan tried unsuccessfully, to convince me that there was nothing more behind the "mom" comment than one of the guys giving him a hard time.

Dan's barrack's room was small, similar to a college dorm room. He shared it with another Recon Marine. The atmosphere seemed a bit like college, too. All of the guys were the same age and were engaged in similar activity. It wasn't like life in the civilian world. There, people interact with many different age groups and types of people who have different ambitions, occupations, and lifestyles. While there are differences amongst the Marines, the similarities far outweigh them. There is a sense of security for many of the guys in the discipline, structure, and "sameness" of the Recon Marine lifestyle. Dan immersed himself in this Marine culture. He was young and inexperienced. He was comfortable in this setting for a short time but would soon be ready to move on.

Family was always important to Dan, but during this time in his life he seemed to distance himself from it. He was committed to spending as much time as possible with his Recon team. The visit from The Madres took second place to activities with his team or particularly, with his team leader. Several times that week, Dan went off on his own with his team leader or other team members and left me to go along with John and his mom.

One morning during our visit, we picked Dan up from his team leader's house. At 10:30 in the morning, Dan calmly sat on the couch drinking a beer. The team leader seemed a bit flustered when we walked in. After all, he was guilty of furnishing beer to a twenty-year-old. Dan was just doing his thing and didn't care that his mother was there to observe it.

One night when we went to a restaurant, Dan ordered a beer. When the waitress asked, he showed her "his" ID and was served the drink. Then he showed me the ID that belonged to one of his friends in Michigan. The friend was two years older than Dan and remotely resembled him. At another restaurant, we had finished dinner and were waiting for our bill. After some time, we finally inquired about it and were informed that the man at the table next to ours had paid for our meal because the guys were Recon Marines. The man had gone outside and seen the Recon sticker on Dan's bike windshield. He came back in and paid our bill.

For most of our visit to California, Dan rode his motorcycle while we drove here and there in our rental vehicle. He had picked up the bike on the first day of our visit and was eager to ride it, at least a few times, before he deployed. In consideration of his engagement and upcoming role of husband and head of his family, Dan decided that he would be safer without the motorcycle, especially in light of the accident he had had with it so soon after he bought it. He sold the bike while he was gone on deployment. For now, though, he rode it whenever he could. It was another way that Dan was establishing his independence and separating from his roots. This was Dan's world, and family was, in some way, an intruder into that world.

On Sunday of our visit, we accompanied the boys to the Escondido United Reformed Church. They attended worship services there when they were in town and able to go. We had dinner with one of the church families who often hosted the young Marines and acted as their family away from home. At least for occasional Sunday dinners, Dan was able to experience a setting closer to what he had grown up in. The boys also took us to a Bravo Company family cookout on the beach. The family dynamics of the Marines in Dan's world were a bit farther from the life in western Michigan where Dan had his foundation. At the end of the week, The Madres returned to Michigan, and the boys were able to focus entirely on preparations for their upcoming deployment.

• • •

In March of 2003, when Operation Iraqi Freedom began, Dan was already enlisted and actively participating in the Delayed Entry Program. However, he was still finishing his senior year of high school and would not enter recruit training until July. His impatience exploded when the original push into Iraq occurred while we were on vacation in Florida. "I should be there! It's happening without me!" he exclaimed over and over. Now, just two and a half years later, he had one deployment behind him and was preparing for his second, which he hoped would include more combat than his first.

Dan's new billet, or job assignment, was as an assistant team leader (ATL). This was quite remarkable considering his youth and inexperience. The responsibilities of an ATL are to assist the team leader in assuring that the five-man team is combat ready. He helps in determining effective tactics to complete any assigned missions. He offers administrative supervision and demands accountability from the five-man team. Dan would be assisting the team leader in planning various patrols, and he would be responsible for adding input to execute those patrols. Dan provided surveillance for the team and was involved in demolition missions. He also helped his team leader on scout sniper missions. He assisted in training the team members to complete all of the assigned missions. In order to assist the team leader in all of these duties, Dan had to be familiar with them and be proficient in them. Dan was excited about the opportunities this billet offered. As an added bonus, the team leader was a qualified scout sniper who was willing to teach Dan what he could and train him as a spotter.

The one drawback to this deployment, was the fact that Bravo Company would be transported by ship. That meant a slow journey. The main objective of this voyage was to deliver the Marines to Iraq, however, so it should not be quite as slow as the MEU had been.

The only exciting thing that happened on the trip to Iraq was Dan's injury. One of the hatches wasn't closing properly. Dan, with his lack of finesse, whammed it with his elbow. In doing so, he caught his arm on the hinge, or something else sharp, and ripped his elbow open. The required half-dozen stitches resulted in substantial ridicule, and also instigated the formation of the PPA, or Price Protection Agency. The goal and purpose of this unofficial organization was to protect and preserve Dan so that he could safely return from the deployment and be married. Dan's teammates took very seriously their commitment to protecting Dan, not only from the "bad guys," but particularly from himself throughout the rest of the deployment.

At the end of the ocean voyage, Dan found himself back in Iraq in much the same conditions as he had experienced on his first deployment. The dust and the desert terrain were the same. Since it was October rather than February or March, the temperatures were a bit warmer. That would change before the deployment was finished. As usual, Dan didn't complain about the conditions or accommodations. He had a job to do, and the surroundings would not affect the completion of any mission. Dan, as the ATL, had a lot of responsibility and would be very busy.

Dan participated in over 100 combat patrols on his second deployment. Not all of them involved direct combat activity. His team completed cache sweeps in which they found and confiscated weapons, ammunition, cash, drugs, or any combination of those items. On three separate occasions, Dan was involved in combat engagements that resulted in the deaths of at least five insurgents.

On one of those occasions, Dan and his team were involved in a mission to catch insurgents who were setting IEDs on the roads in their area of operation. Several members of the team, including the team leader, who was a sniper, set up in a hide site and waited for some activity. As they watched, two guys with AK-47s moved to a location alongside of the road as a convoy approached. When the two guys pulled ski masks over their faces, the sniper in the hide site with Dan shot one of them. The other insurgent fled, and Dan shot M203 grenades, striking and wounding him. The insurgent was killed with the use of a machine gun. That was quite an adrenaline rush for Dan. Any discomfort he may have had with the idea of killing another human being didn't present itself until later.

Dan continued to further his reputation and increase his value to the team. He was smart and quick to assess a situation and come up with a plan of action. He could work independently and be depended on to complete any mission assigned to him. His teammates loved him for his easy-going style and intense work ethic. With just over two years in the Marine Corps, Dan was promoted to sergeant. He had gained the skills that qualified him to act as a team leader in subsequent deployments. Dan's platoon and company command staff encouraged him to pursue commissioning as an officer. The combat experiences still didn't quite satisfy Dan's desire for excitement, but in his mind, things were getting better.

Dan loved to patrol and conduct extended missions in the field where he "became an animal," as he liked to put it. When they were not in the field, though, he was quite bored with day-to-day activities on base. Marines have a way of making their own fun and excitement if none is readily available. Dan had always been quite adept at amusing himself, and his teammates were no different.

They found a little dirt bike that they used to get to various locations around the base. Dan's team knew of his experience with quads and dirt bikes. He had told them many fun stories about riding in the sand dunes. One day, the team talked Dan into trying out the little dirt bike. He hopped on and took off. The guys neglected to tell Dan that there were no brakes on the dirt bike. When Dan was finished showing off how fast it would go and how sharp he could turn at breakneck speed, he prepared to stop in a cloud of dust in front of the guys. He braked and flew right on by them. Much to the delight of the onlookers, Dan finally crashed into a pile of sandbags in order to stop. Obviously, the Price Protection Agency had dropped the ball on this occasion. Perhaps, they were the ones who had started that ball rolling.

Another on-base activity the Marines enjoyed was playing football. Dan was the ultimate athlete. He could run, lift weights, and hike with a pack. He excelled at whatever athletic activity he pursued. However, he had one weakness that the guys discovered when he walked up to a football game in progress one day. Of course, they all clamored for Dan to be on their particular team. They soon found out that Dan was completely inept at anything involving a ball. He could not kick, catch, throw, or hit a ball with a bat. Other than playing a little city recreation league soccer in elementary school, Dan had no desire, experience, or ability to participate in any team sport. He didn't know the rules of team sports. The guys quickly connected this ignorance to his lack of intelligence due to being homeschooled. They had plenty of fuel for their fires of ridicule, which Dan took completely in stride. He dished out more than ample amounts of his own ridicule in return.

When the Marines relaxed on base in the evenings or while out on patrols waiting for something exciting to happen, they told stories about home and growing up. Dan's stories about growing up in small town America and working on the neighbor's pig farm were hard for the guys to believe. For the same reasons the guy at the Recon barracks was surprised to discover that Dan actually had a mom, the guys now had a hard time pic-

Dan at age one, June, 1986.

The perfect Christmas for a future Marine Raider: a wilderness survival book and a 12-gauge shotgun.

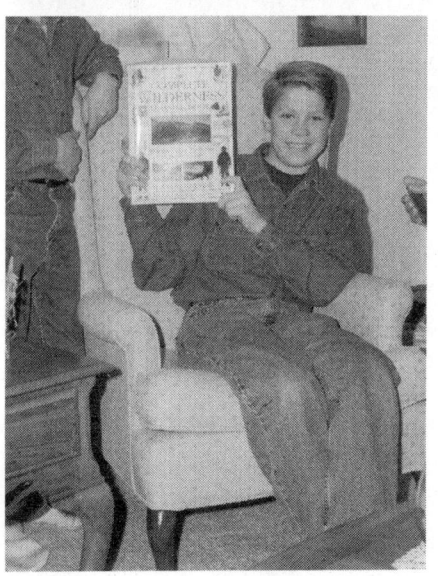

Bottle feeding a prospective 4-H calf at age twelve.

Ross on the left and Dan showing their hogs at the Hudsonville Community Fair in 1996.

Last trip to Florida with the family in 2003. Dan and his rented surfboard.

Dan (standing) with his AR-15, shooting behind a friend's house in Michigan

School of Infantry in 2003.

Scout Sniper School in 2006. Cleaning the sniper rifle.

Playing with snakes on a hike and climbing at Special Operations Training Group Assault Climber School near Bridgeport, California in 2004.

Dan (bottom left) and his survival team at SERE in 2004 with the nest of eggs and snared turkey that would become a legend within SERE.

Dan (right) and John on a California pier in 2005.

Dan with the motorcycle he had for a short time in 2005.

Dan and Basille in Shewan, Afghanistan 2009.

Warrior Dan in combat gear, Afghanistan in 2009.

Hiking at Turkey Run State Park in Indiana following Rebecca's wedding in May, 2010 with Dan, his wife, myself, and Karl.

Karl and Dan make improvements to Dan's landscaping at his newly purchased home in December, 2010.

Dan's funeral.

Karl, Ruth, and Dan's wife.

"25+5" pushup tribute from Dan's brothers-in-arms.

One by one, the Marine Raiders took their jump wings and dive bubbles off their uniforms and placed them on Dan's casket, including the retired Commanding General of Marine Corps Forces Special Operations Command, who took his Two-Star General Officer rank insignia from the shoulder of his uniform and placed it on the casket.

turing Dan as a homeschooled farm boy. They saw his cold and calculated aggression, his extreme focus, intelligent mission planning, and ultimate warrior persona during combat experiences. That image just didn't fit with a farm boy who worked with animals. His teammates saw a Recon Marine, driven by the stress of impending failure to work really hard and excel in every school he entered and every mission he was assigned to. But Dan loved to tell the guys about home. He told the stories with such vivid detail that they felt as though they were there experiencing everything with him. Dan's storytelling revealed a different, deeper dimension that increased the respect his teammates had for him. Along with his many pig farming stories, Dan had 4-H stories to tell.

4-H had been a big part of Dan's childhood and maturing process. Training large animals has its challenges, and Dan told stories about them. The first couple of years that Dan showed 4-H livestock, he spent a lot of time training his animals. He used treats to get his pigs to like him and follow him around. He worked with them almost every day throughout the summer. As he got older, the training methods had to be quicker. One year, about a week before the county fair, Dan announced at dinner that he would be training his pigs that evening. After dinner he went to the barn, closed the door, and proceeded to train his show pigs. Such a commotion and squealing erupted from the barn that it sounded like he was doing great physical harm to the pigs. Pigs squeal for a number of reasons. They may be happy, angry, afraid, hurting, or just ornery. In this case the pigs were angry, becoming ornery, and possibly hurting a little. After about forty-five minutes, Dan returned to the house and stated that the pigs were trained. They were no worse for the experience, and the red marks disappeared before they had to go to the fair. Because Dan understood the personalities of his pigs, he was a good showman. He won the showmanship trophy in two of his 4-H years.

Dan showed beef steers for several years, too. They are a bit larger than pigs and take a lot more time. Dan told the Marines about the quiet Hereford calf he bought to work with his first year. The quiet Hereford rocked the trailer so violently that the truck jostled us all the way home from the farm. The calf made it home and into the pen Dan had prepared. The nylon halter stayed on overnight, since we weren't sure we would ever get it back on the wild thing if it came off. In order to prevent the calf from jumping out of the window in the barn, we tied him so he could comfortably lie down and reach food and water. By the next morning, the halter and lead rope were completely destroyed. The "quiet" calf must have jumped around and spun and twisted all night long. Dan refused to quit even though he was dragged around many times in the ten months of training and preparation. By the time he took the steer to the fair, he could lead him all over the fairgrounds. Dan shared with his teammates that he won third place in Junior Showmanship, but left out the fact that he bawled like a baby when he led the steer that now trusted him to the semi-trailer that would take him away to be slaughtered.

The deployed Marines had what they called "The Jesus Debates." In spite of Dan's sometimes non-Christian behaviors, he was serious about his faith. Even though he wasn't blatant about it with the guys, they knew about it and sometimes asked questions about what he believed. When they did ask, he had ready answers. With time on their hands and not much to do to fill it, many of the guys passed time by reading. *The DaVinci Code* by Dan Brown was very popular, and most of the guys read it. They discussed it at length. One of the resulting questions they investigated was whether or not Jesus was a real historical person. These discussions became known as The Jesus Debates. Dan went to the Bible as the final authority to answer that question. He knew that Jesus was a real historical person, the Son of God who became man to pay the penalty for the sins of His people.

Civilians often feel bad for deployed troops and like to send care packages, especially around the holidays. Although Dan appreciated that, it still somewhat annoyed him. He loved deployments and rarely asked for anything even from his family. The team usually had an overabundance of toothpaste, razors, and many other toiletry items. They always appreciated baked goods which, except for very special baked goods, were shared with the whole team. Occasionally, Dan asked for baby wipes, since that was the mode of cleansing when the team was out in the field for extended periods of time.

During the Christmas season of 2005, a group organized "Project Pillow." The idea was to send pillows decorated by school children or whoever stopped by the "Project Pillow" table display in the malls or wherever they were set up. The pillows were intended to remind the troops that people back home thought about them. They wanted each service person to have a small pillow to carry with them in their pack while out patrolling. While Dan rolled his eyes at this whole idea, he did find a way to use the pillow that he received. Dan's team found a "Charlie Brown" Christmas tree to decorate, and Dan destroyed his "Project Pillow" pillow in order to use its stuffing as snow underneath the tree.

One of Dan's strongest character traits was to have fun in the most uncomfortable circumstances. He didn't care that Iraq was cold and rainy during December or that he had to buddy up in his sleeping bag to keep warm out in the field. He didn't care that he was miles away from home during the holidays. After all, "Home is where I lay my head at night." Dan was surrounded by his team brothers and they celebrated Christmas in fine form with their festive Christmas decorations.

The Price Protection Agency was successful in their endeavor to keep Dan safe for the remainder of the deployment. When Bravo Company returned to California on March 23, 2006, his fiancée surprised him by flying to California to meet him. Together they were able to apply for married benefits and on-base housing, and Dan began to prepare for the next phase of his career. After his fiancée left for Michigan, Dan had very little time to think about his upcoming wedding or marriage. He was scheduled to attend Marine Combatant Diver School in Florida, come home to get married, and return to California to attend Recon Scout Sniper School. It was very difficult to get scheduled for either of these two schools. It was almost impossible to get scheduled for them back to back. The fact that Dan's superiors allowed it is a testimony to their faith in Dan's work ethic and in his ability to succeed. It would be a very difficult program of training to complete, much less to excel at. As always, Dan was up to the challenge.

- 6 -
MARINE COMBATANT DIVER SCHOOL, WEDDING, AND SCOUT SNIPER SCHOOL

Dan was still fairly new to the Marine Corps. He hadn't even been in for three years. Yet, he was about to enter one of the hardest schools in the corps, one which boasted a long waiting list. Marine Combatant Diver School conducts six classes per year and accepts only thirty students for each class. As always when entering a training school, Dan was nervous about not letting anyone down with a poor performance. He didn't need to be concerned. Of the fourteen students that completed the course with him, Dan was the top graduate with a score of 98.22 percent.

Dan began the grueling eight-week course at the Naval Diving and Salvage Training Center in Panama City Beach, Florida on May 2, 2006. The school's mission is to conduct high-risk technical training in the planning, performance, and supervision of amphibious tasks. The students are taught to use surface and sub-surface techniques from naval ships. The skills learned are used primarily in support of Marine Corps reconnaissance and special operations missions. The first couple of weeks in the school included comprehensive medical screening to insure that each student was physically capable to complete the strenuous training. The students learned the fundamentals of diving physics and did a lot of swimming and physical training. During the third week, they gained confidence in the pool and received instruction in the use of SCUBA (Self-Contained Underwater Breathing Apparatus). In the remaining weeks of the course, the students gained knowledge and proficiency in the use of the MK25 Rebreather, which pulls out exhaled carbon dioxide and provides oxygen from a bottle to be used by the diver. It allows for 6-8 hours of dive time and leaves no trail of bubbles for surface detection.

In addition to ground and water physical training and classroom instruction, the students completed approximately thirty-five miles of swimming, fourteen open circuit scuba dives, twenty-four dives using the MK25, and ten open-water swims of 500 to 10,000 yards each. They were tested in areas of drownproofing, underwater knot tying, and a twenty-five meter underwater crossover. Some of the training exercises were the same as, or similar to, what Dan had done in the Marine Combat Water Safety Swimmer Course while in Pre-BRC. The bobbing exercises were now done with hands tied behind their backs and feet tied together. The final exercise was done in the Gulf of Mexico. The students were inserted far out in the open gulf and tied together. They were required to work as a team to complete a complex training exercise.

In addition to the rigors of dive training, Dan kept up with some necessary items in his personal life. In anticipation of his upcoming wedding, he coordinated moving his and his fiancée's belongings to California. One of Dan's Recon teammates used some of his personal leave time and flew to Michigan, helped to load a rental truck with furniture, clothing and personal items, drove the truck to California, and unloaded it all into a storage unit. It was a great relief to Dan to have this help, although it still required a lot of his time. He made a lot of phone calls to make all of the necessary arrangements.

Dan tried to attend church with Tommy, a fellow Recon Marine, each Sunday while he was at dive school. Tommy had been raised in a similar way to Dan. He had been homeschooled until high school, and his father was a minister. Dan and Tommy had some doctrinal differences, which made their church experiences more interesting. They took turns choosing different churches to attend together. After the service, the two Recon Marines critiqued everything about the service: the sermon, the music, the decor, and everything else about the worship experience. Both men grew spiritually through these discussions. They found some crazy churches and even walked out of one before the service was completed. It proved to be more than either of them wanted to sit through.

As Dan came to the end of the Combatant Diver Training Course, the instructors encouraged him to seek an instructor's billet in the school. Dan considered it and decided that a three-year billet as a dive school instructor was not what he wanted to do. He wanted to operate with a team and be eligible to deploy. After the June 20, 2006, graduation from Combatant Diver School, Dan headed home for leave. Next on his packed agenda would be his wedding.

• • •

Dan packed a lot of activity into his trip home. Not only was he going to get married, but he had several things to do in preparation for Scout Sniper School. One of those things was the construction of a "ghillie suit." A ghillie suit is a regulation camouflage uniform with many grass-like strings sewn onto it. The ghillie suit camouflages the wearer as he stalks and hides in grass and brushy areas. Dan wouldn't settle for anything less than exceptional, so his ghillie suit construction was quite labor and time intensive. Dan had hours of work in his ghillie suit. After he used it for Scout Sniper School, he loaned it to another Marine and never got it back.

While Dan was home, he enjoyed some family time, too. One day he, Rebecca, and I went to a Lake Michigan beach. We had a great time swimming, running up and down the beach, and relaxing in the sun. Dan's way of relaxing was constant activity. It was fun to watch him display some of the swimming prowess he had achieved while at dive school. He tried to explain to us how he was, "Sort of able to breath underwater." Neither of us were convinced.

Several of Dan's teammates came to town for his wedding. One young man who had just finished his Marine Corps service told how Dan had saved his life. He and a buddy had gotten into a fight at the barracks. Both had been drinking and were quite inebriated. Dan didn't know either of them but interrupted the fight, calmed things down, and got them both to bed with no serious injuries. This young Marine attributed his turnaround and change of lifestyle to Dan. He went to college and got a degree in social work. His specialty was working with veterans who struggled with PTSD and making adjustments to civilian life. It was obvious during the time he spent in Holland for Dan's wedding, that he loved and highly respected Dan for the impact he had made in his life.

Dan's Marine brothers celebrated alongside of his friends from home. The blending of the two groups at Dan's bachelor party enlightened both groups of friends about who Dan was. After the July 1 wedding and reception, Dan and his bride flew to California on July 3. They left their wedding gifts behind to be picked up later. They had just a few days in California to procure housing, settle in, and prepare for the future before Dan reported to Scout Sniper School on July 7. Usually the Scout Sniper students were required to stay in the barracks. Because of his recent wedding, Dan was given permission to return home most nights. He was sternly warned that if he was late or messed up once in any way, he would be out of the school. The warning was unnecessary. Dan had wanted to become a sniper for a long time and would not let anything, including a new wife, deter his focus.

• • •

Dan attended the Marine Scout Sniper School on Camp Pendleton in Southern California. The school is extremely difficult, and as with every school he attended, Dan was concerned about completing it. Failure was never an acceptable option for him, and he would do whatever it took to accomplish the task. His new bride would have to take a secondary position on his priority list until he finished the course. Even when Dan was home, much of his time was spent studying about the sniper rifle, wind speed and direction, angles, bullet velocity, and everything else involved in long-range shooting.

Dan's homeschool education proved to be very helpful in this school, too. Some of his high school compositions had received admonitions: "To do 11th grade work rather than 6th grade work," and, "Pay attention to punctuation and use complete sentences." He was told, "You show great laziness and lack of effort. If you do not apply yourself more diligently to your schoolwork, you will do no extra curricular activities, like work or trapping after supper." All of the effort that had gone into educating Dan on basic reading, writing, and grammar skills were now brought to fruition as he helped the other students from Recon to write field reports and summaries. Since he was interested in this particular subject, he had no problem applying himself with all diligence.

Snipers must be in excellent physical condition, so naturally, a lot of their training involves PT. A sniper must be able to endure long waits in a "hide" and then get up and move very quickly with no chance to stretch or warm up. He must be able to move undetected in many different environments. Day after day, the sniper students were out on the range working out, stalking, and shooting. They were engaged in night and daytime land navigation exercises. It was so hot during this sniper school session that range time was canceled on some afternoons. At other times, Dan and the other students drank gallons of water to prevent dehydration. When the students stood up after lying in a hide or shooting from a prone position for any length of time, they left a mud puddle from the enormous amounts of sweat that poured from their bodies.

In spite of, or maybe because of the intensity and difficulty of sniper training, Dan loved it. One day, a couple of Marines were at the sniper school for something. One of the guys knew Dan and introduced him to his friend. The friend described Dan as tall, blonde-haired, with a silly grin, sarcastic, a typical Recon guy. What struck him the most about Dan was the fact that he was positive, friendly, and excited about what he was doing in the middle of one of the toughest schools the Corps has to offer. Dan was having fun, and he made the training more fun for everyone around him.

One thing Dan did not enjoy was "field day." On field day, all of the students were required to help clean the classroom. Dan came up with a plan to get out of it. He convinced the other Recon students to approach the sniper instructors and ask for permission to be "thrashed" rather than to participate in field day. The instructors agreed to the plan and proceeded to "torture" the Recon Marines with PT for the next five or six hours. Dan cracked jokes and laughed his infectious laugh which spread to the other Recon Marines. They ended up having a great time and laughed their way through the hours of PT torture. This drove the instructors nearly insane and made the Recon Marines stronger. Even the instructors had to respect Dan's drive and determination. Those Recon Marines are probably the only Marines in the history of Scout Sniper school to have fun every day during the training.

One of the Recon Marines in the Scout Sniper course with Dan had come into it with a bit of an attitude. He had had some problems with his team, his reputation had been tarnished, and he was ready to quit. Dan's influence and encouragement to press on and start over doing the best that he could each day changed his life. He completed sniper school, went back to his team with a different attitude, and re-established his reputation. After he left the Marine Corps, he did some contracting for a few years, then moved to Texas to start a shooting and training facility for handguns and long range rifles. He currently trains military, law enforcement, private security, and civilian individuals to be not only the best shooters they can be but also to be the best people they can be. He attributes much of where he is today to the influence that Dan had on him during sniper training.

In addition to shooting on the range, the Scout Sniper students had to master observation exercises. Using a spotting scope or binoculars, the students looked for ten items in a specifically defined area. The objects were hidden behind brush or other objects. The students had to find at least seven of the items while stalking and remaining hidden themselves. Passing or failing the Scout Sniper course depended, in part, on achieving adequate observation skills and techniques.

The students also had to develop some artistic skills, as they were required to draw field sketches. During these exercises, the students were given one hour to complete a detailed sketch of a particular area or building. Information about the surrounding area, landscaping, target reference points, and possible shooting angles had to be included. The sketches were graded on neatness, correctness, details, and usable information. A score of seventy percent on field sketching was required for the students to pass the course.

The stalking phase of sniper school caused the most anxiety for Dan. He could never sit still. Some part of him was always moving. Stalking had to be done slowly and deliberately without being detected. The students work in what is called a stalk lane with spotters observing from an elevated platform near the lane. If one of the spotters sees movement, they yell, "Freeze!" All of the students must stop where they are and wait for the spotters to direct walkers to the area where the movement was detected.

One day while Dan was struggling to get to a position within a given time period without being spotted, he just stood up and ran over to another spot on the stalk lane. Obviously, the spotters saw him and yelled out the command to "Freeze!" The walkers were directed to the spot where Dan had dropped back down. Although they looked diligently, they could not find him. Somehow Dan escaped detection and got away with his unorthodox movement.

Although Dan didn't have the top scores in Scout Sniper School, he was the graduate whom the instructor's felt had the drive to succeed and be of great benefit to whatever team he served on. He was awarded the Instructor's Choice Award. Similar to his experience in missing the recognition associated with achieving the company high PFT in recruit training, Dan missed out on the recognition he deserved for earning the Instructor's Choice Award in Scout Sniper School. Somehow, even though Dan's name was listed in the program, another student was named and given the award when it was handed out at the graduation ceremony. Afterward, it was all straightened out, and Dan received the award, but not the recognition. Once again, Dan didn't care about the recognition. He was just glad to have graduated and be known as a Recon Scout Sniper. He was completely satisfied with his new military occupational specialty (MOS) of: "8541-Scout Sniper."

We attended Dan's graduation from Scout Sniper School and visited him and his wife in their on-base housing in Southern California. Dan had always loved the ocean. When we vacationed in Florida when he was younger, we spent hours on the beach, studying oceanography, fishing, and playing in the ocean. Dan and his younger brother caught many crabs on the beach by poking a long piece of dune grass in their holes. If a crab grabbed the end of the grass, the boys frantically dug a large hole to uncover the little creature. It was fun to watch the crabs scurry away over the sand in their strange sideways manner. Dan often spotted whales, dolphins, or other sea creatures out in the ocean. The pelicans and blue herons were always looking for a handout.

Dan spent a lot of time surfing with a body board, and on his last visit to Florida with us, he rented a surfboard for a day. Even though the waves weren't real big, he had a great time trying to surf until his foot hit something "hard and rubbery." He was convinced it was a shark. At the time, it was enough to dampen his enthusiasm for surfing. Now that he lived near the ocean, he had renewed his interest in it. He didn't have a lot of time, but he loved hanging out on the beach.

During our brief visit to California to witness Dan's graduation from Scout Sniper School, he took us to the beach and the Oceanside Harbor area. We relaxed and were entertained by a sea lion playing around the boats. Dan seemed quite comfortable in his Southern California Marine Corps environment. Now that the scout sniper training had ended, he could begin settling into the added role of husband and head of his family, as well.

• • •

Two weeks after the completion of Scout Sniper School, Dan and his wife drove to Michigan. They attended the weddings of Dan's Recon friend, John, and Dan's brother. They made the drive from California, rather than flying, in order to take their own wedding gifts back to California when they returned. After the wedding festivities were over, Dan and his wife headed back to California in the evening of October 9, 2006. Dan had a deadline to be back to work in California, and he didn't want to spend money on hotels, so they planned to drive the thirty-six hours straight through. Dan planned that he and his wife could share the driving responsibilities. If necessary, they would stop at a rest area for a couple of hours to sleep.

They drove through the first night and all went well. When Dan became sleepy twenty-four hours into the trip, his wife took the wheel while he slept. In a remote area of Utah on I-70, the little red Saturn hurtled through the black, and now rainy, night at seventy miles per hour. Unknown to either of the occupants, the section of interstate that they were traveling on was notorious for its well-worn tire tracks in the lanes. With the pouring rain filling those tracks, a hydroplane skid was inevitable. Dan's wife was driving with the cruise control, so when the vehicle began to hydroplane, it immediately went out of control. Dan woke up to his wife's screaming. He grabbed the steering wheel and tried to correct the skid, but it was too late.

As the vehicle skidded sideways along the interstate, Dan tucked his wife's head under his arm as well as he could. Then they rode along as the vehicle rolled down the embankment alongside of the interstate. When the vehicle finally came to rest on its top, Dan immediately went into combat defense mode. After two Iraqi deployments, he knew that after an IED attack, the enemy always attacked the disabled vehicle(s) and the occupants with small arms fire. Of course, there was no attack in this instance, but Dan instinctively erupted from the totaled, overturned Saturn to look for it. What he saw instead, were clothes, wedding gifts, and other belongings strewn along the interstate and down the embankment. The Saturn was demolished. Not one piece of its body remained whole and intact. Parts of it marked its path of descent from the freeway.

Dan didn't waste any time wondering what to do. It was after midnight. They were stranded along I-70 in the rain with a demolished vehicle. After checking to make sure his wife was okay, he climbed back up the embankment. The Saturn was too far off the road to be seen by any passersby. Dan hoped that a vehicle would come past on the barren stretch of road so they could get help. He was full of blood from multiple small cuts on his scalp and face. He bled from a small cut on the back of one hand that would require stitches. In his white, blood-stained shirt, Dan stood in the middle of the interstate shortly after midnight, wildly waving his arms at any passing vehicle. His sense of humor surfaced as he imagined the bizarre scene that he presented.

Eventually, someone stopped and called the state police. When the police officer arrived, it was hard to piece together what had actually happened. Apparently, the vehicle rolled several times on its journey down the hill from the interstate. The officer helped Dan locate and secure his handgun. Then they picked up as many of their belongings as they could salvage in the dark. The officer took them to a nearby hospital to be checked out. The hospital personnel and police officer were all very accommodating, especially after they found out that Dan was a Recon Marine. After being served steak dinners by the hospital staff at five-thirty in the morning, Dan and his wife got a couple of hours of sleep in clean hospital beds.

When the small town began to wake up, Dan made plans to get home. The Saturn was sold to a local junkyard for a couple hundred dollars. Dan found a U-Haul rental company, the only transportation rental company in the area, and rented a truck to drive back home. Before leaving Utah and heading for California, the newlyweds returned to the accident scene to gather any salvageable items. Most of the wedding gifts were lost or broken. When they left the scene, Dan noticed that a little further down the interstate, the embankment dropped several hundred feet. They could be thankful that their accident occurred where it did and that their vehicle rolled only 50-60 feet down the embankment after it left the road. Although the car was a total loss, neither Dan nor his wife had been seriously injured.

- 7 -
THIRD DEPLOYMENT AND LEAVING RECON BATTALION

When Dan got back to California with his wife, he debated with himself about what to buy in order to replace his totaled Saturn. He really wanted a pickup truck, but once again didn't want to spend the money on the truck he really wanted. He shopped and researched and talked to everybody he knew about the trucks they were driving. Then he rode his wife's little purple bike back and forth to work at the 1st Recon Battalion for several weeks. He knew that he looked ridiculous and didn't care at all. He had been on a quest for a cool truck since graduating from SOI back in 2003. Dan's first two deployments had come so close together, he had purchased and sold his motorcycle, and he had been at so many different schools. It really hadn't made sense to invest in an expensive vehicle. Now, after weighing the pros and cons again, he bought a decent, used Rav4 for his wife. Dan settled for driving her old Pontiac Sunbird. The truck purchase would wait.

Dan's marriage caused him to think about life differently. He took his responsibility as the head of his home very seriously. His career decisions from now on would affect not only himself, but his wife, as well. He still drank some, but did not drink and party with the guys like he used to. He finally realized that what Mom had been telling him in his early years in Recon was wise counsel. Nobody else had been cautioning him about his behavior. He realized that he could not participate in the lifestyle of most of the Marines and still maintain his faith in God. He had been moving farther and farther from his foundation. He began to make decisions that would help him grow and mature in his faith. Knowing that his wife would need the support of a church family during his many absences for schools and deployments, he sought membership in the Escondido United Reformed Church for himself and his wife.

Dan began to consider where he wanted his career to go. He had many options. Because of his success in different schools he had attended, he was offered multiple instructor billet positions. He was encouraged by his superiors to engage in college level classes in order to pursue commissioning as an officer. Dan considered these options and discussed them with his wife and family. In the end, he decided that he loved what he was doing. He could not understand how getting a college degree in order to be commissioned as an officer would make him a better warrior. He wanted to operate on a team and engage in combat deployments. He wanted to use his qualifications as a sniper and combatant diver. He had advanced to the position of a team leader in 1st Recon Battalion. Dan was smart and understood recon and sniper operations. He was an asset to the team and to the entire platoon.

Because of his attention to detail and understanding of recon operations, Dan had been given the added responsibility of leading the platoon's combat dive team. The dive team was the most technically challenging team in the platoon. In spite of the fact that Dan was younger and had less rank than most of the men, he was selected because of his ability to multitask in stressful situations. Dan had demonstrated calmness under pressure in combat and training experiences, and he exuded that calmness to the rest of the team. He enabled his team to function as efficiently as a well-oiled machine in every situation. Dan knew he was good at what he was doing. He set a high standard by his own example. This motivated everyone around him to better themselves, and in doing so, to better the team.

As his team prepared for their next deployment, Dan examined some of his attitudes about combat. The automobile accident Dan and his wife had in Utah reminded him to think about life and death more seriously. He thought not only about his own life, but also about the lives of those he "hunted."

• • •

Dan had been given a BB gun for his eighth birthday. On a sunny West Michigan morning in early June, he took the new gun outside. The birds sang cheerfully as the sun began to warm the cool, crisp morning air. Dan headed for the barn where the birds were plentiful and began to hunt. Before long, he spotted a sparrow flitting in the rafters. Without a thought, he shot the sparrow. Dan was pretty excited about that first kill, until he was made to think about it.

The death of any creature should not be taken too lightly. I reminded Dan that the sparrow probably had a nest full of babies waiting for food. By the time I told him about the, "Peep, peeping," of the baby birds crying for their mother and starving in the nest, eight-year-old Dan had started to cry. He felt badly about the fact that he might have killed their mother. From then on, he was more careful about the time of year when he shot things. He didn't shoot any more sparrows. Dan didn't lose his love of the hunt or the rush of success, but he gave it more thought.

In Dan's first few years in the Recon Battalion, combat experiences had been an adrenaline rush for Dan and most of the other young men. They had an immature and selfish approach to death, gunfights, and combat. Although the Recon Marines were effective and skillful at what they were doing, the thoughts and emotions that accompanied the experiences were not very healthy. Dan now began to struggle with the idea that the insurgents they were fighting against and killing were men much like himself. They had wives and families. He knew that most of them were Muslims. He believed that when he killed them, he dispatched them to hell—not to seventy virgins awaiting them in heaven, as they thought.

Dan knew that he would have to reconcile his thoughts before facing combat situations again. He could not afford to second-guess his judgment and instinctive actions when he was in the heat of combat. That would endanger his life and the lives of his team members. By seeking wisdom from others and searching the Bible, Dan was assured that God is in control of death and destruction. Dan could not kill anyone before the time appointed by God for their death. None of God's people could be killed and sent to hell before their conversion. Although Dan never took death and his part in the killing of others lightly again, he could do his job confidently without guilt or regret. He still loved what he was doing and enjoyed the challenges that each day presented.

In late May of 2007, Dan departed for his 3rd deployment to Iraq. He left behind a wife. He took along a much more mature approach to all that his job would entail. Dan was happy that he would be flying to Iraq in a cargo plane for this deployment. It would take several days of travel to get there since refueling stops would be necessary. Overall, though, the trip would be much shorter than traveling by ship. The Recon Marines would be free to find a spot in the cargo plane to rest and recline comfortably for the duration of the trip.

Dan's first two deployments had been in the fall and winter. Iraq had been cool and damp. This deployment brought the Marines to Iraq in the summertime. The winter dust that Dan had experienced on his previous deployments paled in comparison to the dry summer dust storms. Daytime temperatures soared to 120-130 degrees. The sun scorched the dry ground and encouraged the wind to scatter the dust. Each hot footstep of every patrol raised a poof of dust that permeated clothing and coated the sweaty skin inside. Nights were somewhat cooler, but still uncomfortably hot. Many of the patrols and missions were executed at night. The Marines struggled to drink enough water to stay hydrated. The water got so hot in their packs that it was difficult to drink. Dan asked for individual packets of Crystal Light peach "iced" tea. Adding them to his hot water made drinking the necessary amount of water somewhat tolerable. Dan didn't complain about the heat or dust any more than he had ever complained about anything. He was focused on the job at hand, and he refused to let anything distract him.

Just a few weeks after arriving in Iraq, Dan's team was part of a convoy traveling through the dark night of June 14. They were on a routine mission. The Marines watched for anything that looked suspicious. Several vehicles were ahead of the one Dan was riding in. Only one remained behind in the string of military vehicles progressing slowly through the Iraqi night. Suddenly, the dark of night exploded in a flash of blinding light and reverberating sound. The last vehicle in the convoy rolled over a pressure-plate IED (Improvised Explosive Device) and caused its detonation. How did all of the vehicles in the convoy miss the pressure plate? How was it that the last vehicle in the convoy set off the IED? Nobody knew, and it didn't matter.

Wasting no time to think about it, Dan leapt from his Humvee and ran to the disabled vehicle. He was the first one to arrive and view the gruesome scene. He knew immediately that the situation was not good. He began to administer emergency first aid. The platoon sergeant asked for his sidearm. Instead, Dan applied tourniquets to his legs. The platoon sergeant was a passenger in the Humvee that had detonated the IED. The explosion erupted underneath the vehicle and drove the metal floor upward. It had severed both of his legs. Not wanting to return home as an invalid, he planned to take his own life with his handgun. Dan and the others on the scene tried to reassure him that he would be okay, but he knew that both of his legs were gone. The team convinced him not to give up. Because of their diligent efforts, his life was saved, and he returned home to recover.

Within two months, he took his first steps on prosthetic legs. When the company returned home from their deployment in November, just five months after the injury, he was able to walk unaided to meet them. He credits Dan's efforts for saving his life and motivating him to continue to fight. After the platoon sergeant recovered from his injuries, he and his wife had their fourth child, a son that would not have been born without Dan's help and encouragement on that dark Iraqi night.

Although Dan was seen as a "fire and forget" Marine, this incident affected him deeply. He kept his emotions deep inside of himself and didn't let them show. His apparent coldness prompted his teammates to assume that he was unaffected by life's circumstances. That was not true, but it was how he operated. One time when Dan was screened for a higher-level security clearance, the psychologist doing the screening offered, "Thanks to your parents and sympathy to your wife," because of the mental strength and emotional detachment that he exhibited. Dan often said that everyone suffers from PTSD. That is true in the civilian world as well as in military life. He believed that how one dealt with PTSD determined how big of a problem it became. Dan didn't let traumatic experiences cloud his judgment or affect his performance.

Dan continued to lead his team for the duration of this deployment. He was quick thinking and creative and kept the enemy constantly on its heels. Day after day, mission after mission, Dan's mastery of team tactics and planning built up his team's confidence. His knowledge of and use of supporting arms made them trust him and love to follow him. His cool demeanor was imitated by the entire platoon, especially in times of high stress. Dan was good at what he did, and he was surrounded by top quality guys who also were good at what they did.

Before this deployment, Dan had always been somewhat afraid of losing limbs or sustaining a debilitating injury in combat. He returned home from this deployment with a different attitude. He was no longer afraid of what would become of him if he sustained an injury. He did his job with the confidence that if he could not continue to operate, he would be productive in whatever he was able to do. Seeing the platoon sergeant survive a devastating injury and experience a dramatic recovery in less than six months had affected the entire platoon. Although the platoon sergeant was not yet fully recovered, he was willing to stay in the fight, and that encouraged all of the men who had served under him to live their lives with the same attitude.

No Stray Bullets

• • •

Dan had been in the Marine Corps for four years. He had deployed three times to Iraq with 1st Recon Battalion. Now, his career was about to take a turn. Dan had enjoyed being a Recon Marine, but there was a new opportunity for him. The Marine Special Operations Command (MARSOC) unit had been established in 2006. MARSOC had its roots in the WWII Marine Raiders, who had been formed to fulfill President Franklin D. Roosevelt's request for a commando-style fighting force with the capabilities to carry out missions on land, sea, and air, and to operate behind enemy lines. It wasn't until 2014 that MARSOC was allowed to take on the designation of the WWII Raiders, but from the resurrection of the unit in 2006, the MARSOC operators unofficially wore Raider patches and considered themselves to be Raiders.

While the Marine Recon Battalion had been limited to working only in the context of Marine operations, the Raiders worked under the authority of US Special Operations Command (USSOCOM). They coordinated their efforts with Navy SEAL and Army Green Beret units. The Raiders also coordinate with NATO Special Operations Forces. The selection process and training to become a Marine Raider is just as rigorous as that of any other special force unit. Their purpose is the same as that of the Green Berets or Navy SEALs. When the unit was resurrected in 2006, a lot of the men Dan had been working with in Recon moved immediately to MARSOC. Dan felt that he needed a little more time and experience in the Recon Battalion. He wanted to wait to see how the new unit would develop and operate before making the switch. After he returned from his third Recon deployment, he was ready to make the move. Dan was proud to be a member of the elite warrior fighting unit with sniper and amphibious assault capabilities known as the Marine Raider Regiment.

Dan agreed to become an instructor in the Special Missions Training Branch (SMTB). Almost immediately upon joining SMTB, Dan was put in charge of organizing a Family Day live-fire event. He was the perfect liaison between the civilian and military world. He had developed a diplomatic style that made everyone think they were getting inside information while he maintained complete confidence with security items. Before his second deployment, Dan had been ordered to give a National Public Radio interview. The command trusted him to do a good interview without saying anything he shouldn't. None of the guys wanted to do it. Dan had only been in the Marine Corps for two years, but he was well-spoken and careful with what he said.

On the family live-fire day, spouses, children and other family members of the 1st Raider Battalion were invited to the range for a day of gun safety and shooting instruction. Dan could be trusted to give excellent professional instruction while making the entire event personal and fun for each participant. While most of Dan's time at SMTB would be spent giving Raider teams final preparatory exercises for deployments, he was up to this first challenge of instructing untrained civilians the discipline of safe gun handling.

Dan was an excellent instructor with a lot of practice. From the time he received his first shotgun for a Christmas gift when he was twelve, he had loved guns. Within just a few years, he had quite an arsenal including an AR-15 and a handgun. In high school, one of the common activities that his group of friends engaged in was target and clay pigeon shooting. Dan was often the one instructing the guys and girls on gun safety and shooting.

One time, after Dan joined the Marine Corps, he and one of his Marine friends planned to teach their wives to shoot. His friend's wife insisted that Dan instruct her. She was terrified of guns and was afraid to shoot one. She didn't think her own husband would have the patience necessary to teach her. As Dan began the teaching session, she had tears streaming down her face. Dan could easily have walked away, teased, or taken advantage of her weakness. Instead, he patiently assured her that she would be okay and continued on with the instruction. He knew when to push, when to lead, and when to come along beside. He knew just how to motivate others to get the job done. Dan's instructional skills made the Family Day live-fire event a safe and beneficial exercise for each family member that participated.

The more important element of Dan's job at SMTB was to design, organize, and evaluate exercises to prepare Raider units for deployment to Afghanistan. Fort Irwin was a perfect location for this training. It is located in the Mojave Desert in northern San Bernardino County, California. Its high desert terrain and climate closely resemble that of Iraq and Afghanistan, the most common deployment destinations for Raider units at that time.

Fort Irwin is about three hours northeast of Camp Pendleton. When SMTB was organizing and running training events, Dan was there for a week or two at a time. During the year and a half that Dan worked with SMTB, he worked hard to coordinate training events that created a realistic environment for Raider teams during deployment certification exercises. MARSOC was a newly resurrected unit and was in the process of developing a deployment certification training program.

As a sergeant, Dan stepped into a billet that would normally be filled by a gunnery sergeant or captain. He excelled in it. He led a four-man evaluation team in their evaluations of the Raider teams at the training facility. He was responsible for preparing and presenting comprehensive evaluations and briefs to Raider commanders. He discussed strengths and weaknesses of the teams in training, and of the training itself. Dan created after action reviews that included videos, photos, and written critiques of every training scenario. In this very challenging billet, Dan's input proved invaluable to the development of the SMTB deployment training program.

The same skill set that Dan had developed when preparing his trapping lines in his youth now came into play. In order to trap on land that did not belong to his family, Dan had to get permission from various neighbors and farmers. He then had to coordinate with other trappers to make sure he didn't overlap their trapping areas. At SMTB he was coordinating things on a much larger scale. He communicated with and coordinated special operations forces, conventional forces, civilian contractors, and federal agency elements. He skillfully weaved all of the elements together in varied and dynamic exercises that improved MARSOC combat readiness. Dan was able to work independently with minimal oversight. This allowed the higher command to focus on other areas of training and deployment preparations. He was self-motivated. When he noticed gaps in the training, or in the personnel required to accomplish the training, he stepped in to fill those gaps. He gained an extensive knowledge of request procedures at Fort Irwin.

On one training rotation, Dan worked alongside the operations chief from 2nd Marine Raider Battalion. The master sergeant utilized Dan's expertise to establish training requirements and help him work through the request procedures for range and training areas at Fort Irwin. Because of his knowledge of the multiple layers of request procedures, Dan was able to identify potential problems, answer any questions, and schedule live fire ranges. This allowed 2nd Raider Battalion to complete their warrior training before deploying to a combat zone.

Any Marines who have completed jump school are required to re-qualify periodically. Dan made sure he was aware of any jump re-qualifications that were necessary for particular teams coming to Fort Irwin for pre-deployment training. He then coordinated air support that enabled all of the jumpers at 1st SMTB to re-qualify while they were there. Each one was able to accomplish necessary refresher airborne training before leaving for upcoming deployments.

In reward for his outstanding performance as assistant operations chief and for his assistance to the air officer of 1st SMTB, Dan was recommended for and received the Navy and Marine Corps Achievement Medal. Dan had been instrumental in the development of the training program. In doing so, he had improved the combat readiness of deploying Raider forces.

One of the things that enabled Dan to accomplish so much in the coordination of training events was his ability to work well with those he was training, as well as with their commanders. His ability to market himself and get along with different types of people began when he showed his 4-H livestock. An important part of raising 4-H market animals is getting bidders to the auction to purchase your animal. The more bidders you have, the more profit you will have from your project. Dan was really good at figuring out how to deal with the different types of businessmen who might be interested in buying his animals. Some of the buyers were looking for a very professional salesman and showman. Others enjoyed joking around and having a good time with the 4-H members. Many were somewhere in between. Dan could be any type of salesman that the buyer liked.

The first year that Dan had a steer, he was a little concerned about finding a buyer. By the time a steer goes to the fair, the 4-H member has a substantial financial investment in him, in addition to the time invested. Not many small business owners are willing to open their wallets for the amount of cash it takes to reward a 4-H member adequately for his time and effort. Dan went to work and contacted many buyers. He focused particularly on the owner of a local western store who had purchased steers at previous fairs. Although Dan had no connection to him, and the business owner had no reason to be interested in purchasing his steer, Dan worked hard to establish a relationship with him.

Bill was a buyer who liked to have a lot of fun, and Dan had a lot of fun with him. He became a frequent visitor in the western store and always stopped to say, "Hi," to Bill. Dan often updated him on the growth and progress of his steer. During the week of the fair, prior to the 4-H livestock auction, Dan kept his eyes open for Bill. Whenever he saw him, he asked if Bill had seen his steer in the barn. Dan told him that his was by far the best steer at the fair that year.

On auction night, Bill was there, but he left before Dan's turn in the sale ring arrived. Dan was disappointed, because he had hoped that Bill would be his buyer. When Dan got into the ring with his steer, the price rose slowly at first, but then it started increasing more rapidly. What Dan didn't know was that before he left, Bill had given his buyer number to a friend of his and told him to, "Buy that kid's steer!" The friend asked how high to go on it, and Bill told him again, "Buy that kid's steer." The friend got another friend involved and together they decided how much of Bill's money to spend on Dan's steer. Dan was the happy recipient of the proceeds of a good-natured practical joke played on Bill. In addition to being an amusing story, it demonstrates how likeable Dan was.

His professionalism and ability to get along with peers and superiors alike were very helpful attributes. In his work in SMTB at Fort Irwin, Dan used those characteristics and abilities to get range clearances and any other unit cooperation he needed to effectively set up his training exercises.

In between the SMTB training rotations that Dan was orchestrating at Fort Irwin, he completed several schools. In September of 2008, he took a six-week Sergeant's Course. Dan wasn't too excited about this school, but he had to do it if he wished for any future promotions. He was assigned the responsibilities of Class First Sergeant, which gave him daily accountability for the eighty-four students in the class. He received a NCO (Non-Commissioned Officer) sword at graduation as a reward for being the class honor graduate. In February of 2009, just five-and-a-half years after entering the Marine Corps, Dan was promoted to Staff Sergeant. Wherever Dan was and whatever he was doing, it seemed that he jumped into the lead and exceeded all expectations.

In the spring of 2009, Dan completed the Marine Corps Special Operations Breacher Course and the Advanced Special Reconnaissance Course. In the breacher course, Dan learned a lot about explosives and breaching different types of barriers, doors, and gateways. He enjoyed blowing stuff up, and now he was learning to do it more efficiently and effectively. It was a fun course for him. The advanced reconnaissance course prepared him for more leadership in mission planning and combat operations. He was hoping to obtain a position on a Raider team when he left SMTB. This course would help him move in that direction. Dan was able to take those two courses consecutively in North Carolina with a three-day break in between.

Dan convinced us to spend the extended weekend with him. He was staying in a Holiday Inn Express in Snead's Ferry, North Carolina, a sixteen hour drive from our house. Karl, Rebecca, and I left early on a Thursday and returned home late the following Monday. Dan was so eager for us to arrive at his hotel that he kept calling to follow our progress from Michigan to North Carolina. He planned to order a pizza when we arrived and claimed to be, "Completely giddy," about hosting us in his hotel room. He made it a point to make friends with the housekeeping staff of any hotel he stayed in. It served him well on many occasions. In this instance, he was able to acquire two trundle beds, at no cost, to add to the queen bed in his room. We were a bit crowded, but had loads of fun. It was worth any inconvenience to spend Friday through Sunday with him. We drove around together and did some sightseeing. We spent a little bit of time at the ocean and checked out some city parks. Dan took us to Camp Lejeune and showed us the new MARSOC headquarters that was under construction at that time. It was obvious that he was very proud to be part of this elite special operations unit.

- 8 -
SHEWAN

Dan had enjoyed instructing the teams at SMTB, but he would rather have been doing the training and preparing for deployments himself. In July, 2009, he was excited to be assigned to a Raider team from Alpha Company that planned to deploy in August. They needed one more man to complete their team. With only a month to prepare and get to know his new team members, Dan had a lot to do. He had missed all of the pre-deployment workups and training, but still decided to take a week of pre-deployment leave in Michigan to see friends and family.

When Dan returned to California, it didn't seem to matter that he was new to the team or that he had missed the team preparations. His reputation from 1st Recon Battalion and the Special Operations Training Group had preceded him. He had worked with some of the command personnel from Alpha Company on previous Recon deployments or at SMTB. They vouched for him and that hastened his orders to join the team. Nobody doubted Dan's ability to fit in with and be an asset to the team. Many of the guys knew of him or had experienced training under him at SMTB.

As a young child, Dan had not been very brave. In fact, one of the family's favorite camping stories involved sitting around the campfire in a very civilized state park campground enjoying the reading of *True Bear Tales*, a book by David E. Young, a ranger in Porcupine Mountain State Park. As twilight waned and it began to get dark, Dan suddenly interrupted to ask if it was time for bed. That was completely out of character for him, but he insisted that he was tired and we should go to bed. It turned out that he was afraid of an imminent bear attack and wished to be safely tucked in his sleeping bag inside the camper. A brief fifteen years later, Dan was no longer a fearful child. He had three combat deployments and multiple high-level military training schools on his list of achievements. He was confident, physically and mentally strong, and calm at all times. His calm demeanor was especially evident in stressful situations. Dan was hard-working, unselfish, and competent. He would have a positive impact on any team he joined.

Alpha Company deployed in early August and arrived at FOB (Forward Operating Base) Heredia in Farah Province. They would be working to establish a new FOB near the city of Shewan in the Bala Baluk district of Farah Province, located in western Afghanistan. Shewan was a known safe-haven for insurgent activity. It was an important objective because of its strategic accessibility to supply lines into the Bala Baluk region. With this daunting objective before them, Dan's team members awoke on the first morning in Afghanistan to his insistent knocking on their doors. Dan collected each one of their M-4 rifles, which were painted a solid desert sand color, and proceeded to repaint them all with his own favorite "laundry bag camouflage" pattern. This would serve to break up the solid color which would stand out in the shifting sands of the desert as the team sought to position themselves for action without being detected. It was a small thing, but was a huge statement of the contribution that Dan would make to the team. He was always thinking about the success of the missions and the safety of the team.

Dan's team was quick to appreciate his efforts, but they became a little apprehensive about his background when he received some pictures from his family. Dan had sent a few pictures of his team by way of email. We decided to send him some pictures of our own team. We had great fun posing in menacing positions with our rifles and shotguns in the driveway of our home. When Dan received the pictures, he showed them to a few of his teammates. They quickly wondered what kind of a family he came from. It is a little strange that they should question Dan's family. Each one of them, in their own way, were a little quirky. Dan, too, had some crazy ideas and obsessive/compulsive tendencies that made him seem just a bit insane. In the beginning, they didn't know Dan very well, and they didn't know what to think about his gun-toting family members. By the end of the deployment, many of Dan's new teammates had discovered that he was an exhausting person to be around. They observed his boundless energy and never-ending arguing. They decided that he was a little out of the ordinary. The pictures of his family may have helped to explain some of his idiosyncrasies.

Dan was excited about this deployment. As the operations SNCO (Staff Non-Commissioned Officer), Dan's duties would include assisting the team leader and team chief in planning all combat operations. It looked like there would be plenty of them. The new FOB began as a tent camp in the middle of a wasteland of insurgents. There were a few civilians living in the town of Shewan, but they were under the domination of the insurgents. The FOB was surrounded by a fence or wire. As long as the Marines stayed on their side of the road, inside the wire, there was no trouble. If they left the wire or crossed the road, they were fired upon. Over the course of the deployment, Dan participated in many patrols, reconnaissance missions, direct action raids, and one prolonged combat operation. The combination of these operations resulted in many enemies killed and thousands of pounds of explosives being removed from insurgent possession.

The prolonged combat operation, known as Operation Red Thunder, took place in early September. It was a seven-day operation to clear the insurgents out of Shewan. Day after day, Dan's team, MSOT (Marine Special Operations Team) 8111, along with the Afghan National Army (ANA), picked away at the enemy stronghold. Multiple reconnaissance patrols met with a determined enemy force. During one reconnaissance mission, Dan was on a rooftop providing cover fire to a maneuvering unit below him. He realized he was pinned down when each time he poked his head up to provide cover fire, a Taliban sniper took shots at him. Dan continued with his sniper cover, and eventually the engaged ground unit was able to maneuver to a position of dominance. The area was secured, or at least the team thought it was. When Dan headed down a stairway to get off the roof, shots again rang out. Bullets hit the wall behind him. Even as he ducked, he spotted the gunman. It was a member of the ANA, who was supposed to be on the same side as Dan. One of Dan's teammates was frantically motioning to the shooter, indicating that Dan was one of their own, so stop shooting at him. Dan laughed about the incident and was thankful that, at least on this occasion, the ANA were not very good marksmen.

During the efforts to clear Shewan, the team was attacked at various times with rocket propelled grenades. One day, a supply truck drove up to Dan, and the driver began to ask some questions. Dan stood about fifteen feet from the truck and suddenly heard, *Tingly, tingledy, ting, ting,"* coming toward him on the gravel street. An RPG (Rocket Propelled Grenade) zipped down the road between him and the truck. Dan didn't waste time to answer the driver's questions, but told him, "I don't really know, but if I were you, I would move out of this area." Without hesitation, the driver took his suggestion and drove off. Dan was often the comic relief needed in combat situations to loosen everybody up and enable them to operate calmly and efficiently.

MSOT 8111 encountered indirect fire, sniper fire, IED's, and small arms fire. While preparing for one patrol, the Raider team realized that they were seriously outnumbered by the enemy force they were about to encounter. In an effort to encourage the team, Dan looked around their huddle and stated confidently that they had six guns and could claim victory with them. The other guys looked around the circle, did their own counting, and told him they had seven guns. Dan sheepishly counted again, included his own gun this time, and stated, "Well, seven is even better than six, especially when it comes to our guns!"

During these engagements over five days of fighting, MSOT 8111 had killed at least seven enemy forces. Yet, they had been unable to diminish the enemy's resolve and determination. On September 12, 2009, MSOT 8111 led the ANA forces, as they began Day 6 of Operation Red Thunder. Their objective for the day was to protect two convoys passing through the area. The convoys each contained over fifty vehicles. They carried resupply items for remote ANA outposts and food that was desperately needed by the local population.

Dan was the gunner for the Remote Weapon System MK-19 in one of three light-armored vehicles called RG-33 vehicles. The MK-19 is a grenade launcher capable of shooting 40–60 rounds per minute with a kill zone of five meters and a wounding zone of fifteen meters from the point of impact. It was mounted on top of the vehicle. The Remote Weapon System allows the gunner to engage targets by using a TV screen and joystick from inside the vehicle. When Dan was in middle school and high school, he had seen absolutely no point in wasting time playing video games or doing anything else on a computer. He had more important things to do. In his Marine Corps career, he used computers extensively. On this combat mission, he was instrumental in playing a "life and death video game." Since the MK-19 Remote Weapon System is intended to be used from inside the RG-33, there is no armor or protection around the weapon mount. It is possible, however, to disengage the weapon from the remote system and operate it manually from on top of the vehicle. The gunner in that situation, is completely unprotected.

By six that morning, the three MSOT 8111 RG-33 vehicles were in position to provide quick reaction force protection for the ANA company who would be securing the road for the convoys to pass through. At seven, the predictable ambush began with small arms fire directed toward MSOT 8111 and the ANA that protected the road. The Taliban insurgents were determined to prevent the convoys from delivering the important resupply items. The ambush intensified as the first convoy moved through the area, and the ANA forces became pinned down by heavy enemy fire that covered two kilometers of the road. MSOT 8111 moved in to support the ANA. Small arms fire and rocket propelled grenades came from compounds and fence lines 30-300 meters from the road as MSOT 8111 moved in closer to assist. Enemy fire impacted all around the vehicles.

As the fight intensified, the optics on the remote weapon system in Dan's vehicle were disabled by enemy fire. The team chief riding with him exclaimed, "We need to get that gun back!" Dan, without any thought or hesitation, was already climbing to the top of the vehicle to manually operate the MK-19. Dan's quick action resulted in killing several enemies and suppressing enemy positions, allowing the first convoy to get through the kill zone. Dan's continued efforts enabled the wounded Afghans to be evacuated.

The second convoy was scheduled to pass through, and the enemy renewed their determined efforts to prevent its passage. Their small arms and sniper fire was honing in on its intended targets. Every side window in the MSOT RG-33 vehicles were shot out. Dan maintained his unprotected position even after his own vehicle was impacted by a rocket propelled grenade that stunned its occupants. When the second convoy began to pass through the kill zone, the Afghan national drivers panicked and abandoned their vehicles. This resulted in a traffic bottleneck in the road.

From his position atop the vehicle, Dan saw a US vehicle get hit by an 83MM recoilless rifle shot. A US soldier in the vehicle was critically wounded. Dan directed the maneuvering of his vehicle to support the evacuation of the US army troop. As his team members dismounted under heavy fire to help with the evacuation, Dan continued to provide effective cover fire to protect them. He was able to kill several of the enemy who exposed themselves in trying to target the casualty evacuation efforts.

Dan continued to keep the enemy somewhat suppressed while he relayed the location of high enemy concentrations to the Joint Terminal Attack Controller. His firing of the MK-19 kept the enemy down long enough for the Joint Terminal Attack Controller to employ air support from a B-1 bomber. While waiting for the airstrike, Dan remained in his exposed position and communicated to US Army and ANA personnel on the ground to take cover. The impending air strike would target enemy positions less than a hundred meters from their positions. This allowed the dropping of two GBU-38 bombs, which killed a high concentration of enemy personnel with no damage to friendly elements. The air support eliminated the enemy positions and allowed the team to break contact with the enemy at the Shewan Garrison.

In the course of this conflict, enemy fire had struck the MK-19 with at least six precision rounds. The impacts destroyed the thermal sight and caused fragmentation to spray from it. Dan had to disassemble and reassemble the weapon several times, under fire, in order to clear malfunctions caused by these impacts. His calm under fire and knowledge of the weapon system had enabled him to keep the vital weapon system in the fight.

The day was not quite over for MSOT 8111. They gathered at the Shewan Garrison to regroup. It was discovered that the vehicle weapon systems were nearly out of ammo, the vehicles had multiple flat tires, and all of the windows had been shot out. Dan organized the team to get the tires changed and divide up the remaining ammo. The team leader coordinated with higher command. Dan determined what resupply items were necessary to continue the mission and selected a suitable drop zone to receive them. When the team was informed that a US service member from another unit was possibly missing in action in the area, Dan immediately volunteered to resume his exposed position as the team moved toward enemy contact to find and retrieve him.

After twelve hours of engagement, four of which involved very intense fighting, 30–40 enemies were killed in action. Six ANA soldiers and two US Army troops were also killed in the action. Dan had remained in his exposed position for much of the engagement. He was not only still alive, but was completely unscathed.

For his part in this particular mission, Dan received the Bronze Star Medal with combat distinguishing device. He was recognized for having "immeasurable value to MARSOC and the Special Operations Community as a whole. His steadfast leadership, selfless attitude, tireless work ethic, and the proactive manner in which he accomplished his mission have made him directly responsible for the high level of mission success that MSOT 8111 enjoyed. His tenacity and devotion to MSOT 8111's mission success is unmatched."

Even though Dan didn't make a big deal about it, we could tell that he was pretty excited about receiving the Bronze Star Medal. When he was finally presented with the Bronze Star Medal in 2011, he didn't let anyone know when the ceremony would take place. He didn't want anyone to adjust their schedules or spend money flying to California to acknowledge his achievement. We had been privileged to observe the presentation of a Bronze Star Medal at the time of Dan's graduation from recruit training and had to content ourselves with that memory. Dan's humility prevented us from being able to observe and honor him at the presentation ceremony.

Dan's quick thinking in combat was indicative of his quick thinking nature. He could devise a plan in almost no time, and with almost no thought, whenever he was in a tight spot that required "out of the box" thinking. As early as the first year he possessed a driver's license, Dan had demonstrated how quickly he could get out of trouble. Michigan winters can be quite intense with heavy snowfall and slippery roads. One snowy winter evening, Dan headed out to meet friends. As he attempted to make a left turn at a rural intersection, he realized that he was driving too fast and would not be able to make the turn. It was too late to go straight, so as he headed toward the ditch, he straightened the wheels and hit the gas. He entered the ditch with enough speed to get through the ditch and into the field on the other side of it. He maintained his speed and drove toward the access driveway at the other end of the field. Dan was able to re-enter the road without getting stuck. It was a good thing that the field was frozen underneath the snow, or his "quick thinking" could have resulted in burying him in the mud, far out in the field.

• • •

Although Dan loved what he did, he didn't believe that any of the military efforts in the Middle East would make a long-term difference. The people of Iraq and Afghanistan have an entirely different mindset that can't be changed by changing the government, leadership, or environment. One thing that particularly bothered Dan was the position of women in Iraqi and Afghani society. He saw that women were viewed as possessions, like

American dogs. Some dogs are treated well, and some are not. Regardless of how it is treated, each one is still just a dog. With that in mind, the change of direction in the 2009 Shewan deployment after the completion of Operation Red Thunder was a welcome one.

The Taliban insurgency had discovered that the Marines of MSOT 8111 were not to be trifled with. Things calmed down substantially, and FOB Meadows began to take shape. With the new focus of the deployment, Dan became instrumental in coordinating and supervising the building operations. Much of his experience in the building trade had been acquired in his youth while helping his grandpa and dad work on projects in the house and barn. Grandpa was retired, and because the boys were homeschooled, they were often available to help with various jobs. If Grandpa called to say he was going to come and work on something, the boys hurriedly finished up whatever minimal schoolwork was absolutely necessary. Then they wrapped their nail aprons twice around their tiny waists, hung their hammer holders from their belts, and spent the afternoon pounding nails or "gophering" for Grandpa. They learned a lot about building things. Even more beneficial was the quality time they spent with their grandfather.

On the FOB, Dan worked tirelessly. Every morning he was up with the sun, running the bobcat or some other tool or equipment, while his teammates attempted to sleep. "Dan," they would say, "There are no pigs to slop, no chickens to feed, no cows to milk. Stay in bed!" He would laugh and retort back that they were wasting daylight. He occupied himself for hours making plywood toilet seats. He adjusted and reworked them until they met with his comfortability standards. He built a laundry area in the middle of the dust. Since it never rained, he didn't bother to enclose it. The laundry area consisted of a washer and dryer set on a wooden platform. At the end of each day, Dan was tired and went to bed long before the other guys. He was then ready to face the next morning much earlier than they.

Dan was in charge of hiring Afghan locals from the village of Shewan to do much of the actual labor. One of them, Basille, acted as foreman. He spoke broken English and was the liaison between Dan and the other workers. Much communication transpired between the two. Basille would often knock on the door of the team's housing facility to ask Dan questions about something. Whoever answered the door would automatically defer it to Dan with, "Dan, your boyfriend is here."

The hired Afghan workers didn't always accomplish tasks up to Dan's specifications. One day, after they had hung a gate, Dan noticed that it didn't swing very freely, and it hung rather haphazardly from its frame. He hooked a chain to it and pulled it off its hinges with the bobcat. Then he made the laborers do it over again. Basille was very impressed with Dan's prowess in driving the bobcat. One day he asked, "Meester Dan, you are so goot with driving the 'brobcat'. Do you drive the aeroplane, too?" That, of course, gave the team a bit more ammunition with which to tease Dan. He just laughed and shook his head. Then he continued on about his business.

One day, all of the hired Afghan laborers came to Dan and indicated that they were not getting paid enough for the work they were doing. If Dan wouldn't pay more, they would not return to work the next day. Rather than to respond immediately, Dan went to ask the Afghan interpreter if they were being paid a fair wage. When he found out that they were receiving a very fair amount, he went back to them and told them that they didn't have to come back at all. He planned to go into the village and find others who were willing to work. With great animation, they exclaimed that they would continue to work for the previously agreed upon wages.

Throughout this entire deployment, Dan had been responsible for the property assigned to the team. As the deployment came to its end, he was accountable for over $30 million worth of serialized items. He would be responsible to see it transported back to the states, transferred to the company that would be replacing his at FOB Meadows, or accounting for its necessary disposal. It was a huge responsibility, but in the scope of what had transpired and what had been accomplished by Alpha Company on this deployment, it was just "stuff."

- 9 -
CHANGES IN CAREER AND PERSONAL LIFE

Dan returned home to California in late January, 2010. His only sister was planning to get married in May, and she really wanted to have Dan visit one last time while she was still living at home. Proving that he was an awesome big brother, Dan came home to Michigan for a post-deployment leave in February. He and his wife came to Michigan again in May for the wedding. Dan and Rebecca had always had a very close relationship. Dan's willingness to pay for two trips home to make her happy confirms it.

When they were young, Dan often engaged in tea parties and make-believe games with Rebecca and her dolls and stuffed animals. That wasn't because Dan enjoyed it so much but rather because Rebecca enjoyed it. He always spoiled her, simply because she was his little sister. Dan was extremely silly and imaginative. Many nights at bedtime, the kids would giggle and carry on upstairs until they were sternly instructed to, "Knock it off." Almost always, Dan was entertaining the other two kids with stories and antics with his Teddy bear, Ted. He brought Ted to life by moving and talking for him. It was ridiculous and funny, because of who Dan was, even as a youngster.

As an adult, Dan still tried to humor Rebecca. He did his best to eliminate any disappointments for her that he could. One day while he was home in February for his post-deployment leave, Dan and Rebecca had plans to go for a run. The morning dawned cold, rainy, and miserable. It was a typical February day in Michigan and did not look like a good day for running outside. Rebecca was almost in tears. She had been looking forward to running with Dan so much. Dan, still the adoring big brother, wanted to fix everything and take care of the weak and needy. He suggested that they run together on the treadmill. One can only imagine how that went. Rebecca ran in front with Dan behind her. It didn't work out very well or last very long. It did, however, provide a precious memory of the silliness they shared.

In May, Dan and his wife came back to Michigan to help out with Rebecca's wedding. Dan used the computer and PowerPoint skills he had acquired in making reports at SMTB, to put the wedding video together. He was meticulous about getting the music just right. He was always meticulous about everything. Rebecca wanted to use one song for her pictures, another song for her fiancé's pictures, and another song for the pictures of the two of them together. Dan wasn't happy with just fading in and out from song to song. He worked for hours to eliminate verses or phrases to make the songs end just right with the pictures.

When it was time to play the video at the wedding ceremony, Dan demonstrated his "calm under fire" demeanor. At first, the music didn't play at all. Dan fiddled with this and that. After several minutes, he realized that everyone was watching him and waiting with bated breath. He calmly stated, "There is supposed to be music with this." Then he went back to his tinkering. Sensing his calm and confident attitude, everyone relaxed. A few seconds later, he found the correct button and presented an almost flawless PowerPpoint program—with sound.

After Rebecca's wedding, Dan and his wife took a few extra days to relax and do some hiking with Karl, myself, and my parents at Turkey Run State Park in Indiana. Dan helped to pack and prepare for the trip. He made the mini-vacation memorable for all of us. It was a wonderful opportunity for him to spend extended time with his grandparents. Other than brief visits, Dan had been away from the family for several years. He was able to observe them for three days and realized that they were not nearly as active and able as he remembered. We enjoyed sunny skies and seventy-degree temperatures at the southern Indiana state park. We hiked through the woods, in rocky creek beds, and up sandy cliffs. My parents enjoyed the warmth of the sun from a bench or sidewalk and stayed close to the lodge. They could no longer hike as they had years ago when we camped with them with our little kids.

Dan particularly enjoyed an episode with raccoons in the back of our truck. One evening, we were relaxing in the lodge after a day of hiking. One of the lodge employees came in and asked if we owned the gray truck in the parking lot. When we said that we did, she told us that raccoons were enjoying whatever we had in the pickup bed. Dan flew out of the lodge, leaped down the stairs, and ran to the truck. Karl and I, along with Dan's wife, hurried behind. We chased the raccoons out of the truck bed. Dan favored us with his huge laugh, as one of the raccoons escaped down a storm drain with a giant *kersploosh!*

In the summer of 2010, Dan and his wife purchased a home in San Marcos, California. Up until then, they had lived either in on-base housing or in a rented apartment. Dan had been happy with that arrangement. He wasn't home much and didn't want to spend time with the consuming responsibilities of home maintenance, yard care, and everything else that goes with home ownership. His wife really wanted to have her own place to paint and decorate as she wished. Dan complained some about his new responsibilities after moving into their new home, but in reality, he had a lot of fun working in the yard and making improvements to his new property. Years ago, when he worked on the pig farm, his boss had told him, "Happy wife, happy life." He believed it back then. Now he experienced its truth.

Ever since he had gotten married, Dan was conscious of how much money they spent. Now that he owned a home, he was even more aware of how expensive things were. When the spending "merry-go-round" got out of control, Dan went into what he termed "poverty mode." In poverty mode, he spent no money on anything that was not absolutely necessary. He insisted that his wife go into poverty mode with him. No going out, no buying anything, just living in poverty until the finances balanced out again. Although owning a home did cost more money than renting, and poverty mode occurred more often, it was good for Dan to have a house to pour his energy into. He loved to be busy, and there was always something to tinker with in the house or yard.

At the battalion, Dan had become an element leader on his Raider team. He was directly accountable to the team leader and team chief and aided them in conducting various training exercises. The teams had the opportunity to engage in urban training with the Los Angeles Police Department Special Weapons And Tactical units. That was a pretty intense and eye-opening experience for men who had seen a lot of combat on foreign soil. Working with the SWAT teams allowed them to experience an entirely different type of combat zone on their home turf. It also exposed Dan to the world of law enforcement, which might be a viable second-career option after military service.

Dan was able to complete many advanced training courses during 2010. The MMPC (Multi Mission Parachute Course) qualified him as a free fall parachutist. It was a lot more technical and a lot more fun than the basic jump course at Fort Benning, Georgia, which he had completed in 2003. MMPC was conducted in Arizona. The clear air and generally sunny skies in southern Arizona make it a perfect location for high altitude parachute training. The MMPC students learned what is known as HAHO (High Altitude High Opening) and HALO (High Altitude Low Opening) parachuting skills. The technology is astounding.

The parachutists in HAHO jumps are able to jump from up to 35,000 feet above the ground. They are able to land in a very specific location up to forty miles away from the jump location. The jumpers use GPS systems to determine their location and destination. They steer and control the jump and landing by making small changes in the position of their parachute. In HALO jumps, the students fall freely through the air for over a minute. They reach a very high rate of speed and learn to control their fall by using very tiny body movements. Dan was excited that he would no longer have to do any qualifying jumps as a "lawn dart."

Most of the training that Dan received now was pretty intense. It was also labeled as high security or classified. He wasn't able to share the knowledge he gained with civilians. He reflected on the fact that his friends at church had no clue what he actually did for a living. Even though he was the same person in all situations, he necessarily led two separate lives. He knew that because he hunted and killed men for his life's occupation, he would never again be content to hunt animals as many of his friends back home in Michigan did. Dan's combat and field expertise had reached a level that was sought out even by the Commanding General of MARSOC. On random occasions, Dan was called to his office to share a drink. The general asked for suggestions, guidance, and advice about special forces operations. Dan was seen as "one of the best of the best" by subordinates, peers, and higher command personnel.

In December of 2010, Karl and I met Dan and his wife at the Grand Canyon. Dan had suggested the trip and did almost all of the planning and organizing. On Wednesday afternoon when we arrived at the hotel Dan had reserved, he promptly took charge as the tour guide for the next two days. From the time that Dan was a young teen, he had gradually assumed more and more leadership in our relationship. As he gained knowledge and experience as a teen on the pig farm, he helped with maintenance at home and in the barn. He was a big help in the 4-H club and with our family's 4-H animals. He helped with a lot of things that required more strength than I had. Now, after all of his world travel and life experiences, he was more than qualified to take the lead in most situations. He had a confident way about him that made everyone think that he had all of the answers (whether he actually did or not) and that he could handle whatever happened (whether he could or not). At the same time, he valued our insight and wisdom in some of life's deeper realms more than he ever had before.

Dan drove us through four inches of slushy snow and fog for most of Thursday morning. The cloudy, drizzly day limited our sightseeing opportunities into the Grand Canyon. We enjoyed a different sort of beauty than sunshine and clear skies would have offered. Late in the morning, the sun came out and burned the fog away. The rest of the day was clear and cold, and we experienced the Grand Canyon's beauty all over again.

On Friday morning, Christmas Eve, we left the Grand Canyon and followed Dan and his wife to their home in California. Dan kept us busy for the next ten days at his new residence. I did some yard and landscape work while Dan and Karl worked on several home improvement projects. One sunny, warm day, Dan drove the four of us to the Cedar Creek Falls hike. From the parking area, we hiked down a dry rocky area into a gully-like valley. The trail meandered up and down over the craggy rocks and hills. As we neared the creek, the vegetation became more lush and green. When we reached the freezing cold knee-deep creek, we took our shoes and socks off, rolled up our pants, and plunged ahead. Dan's wife missed out on that exhilarating experience, because Dan carried her across the creek. We continued to follow the creek's course up to Cedar Creek Falls. After snacking and resting in the beauty of the falls, we started on the nearly four-mile hike back to the parking area. On the way, we all realized that the way into the valley was, in spite of its ups and downs, mostly downhill. That meant that the way out of the valley was mostly uphill. We were all contentedly sore and tired when we reached our vehicle in the parking area.

• • •

After we left for Michigan in January of 2011, Dan finished his preparations for the Advanced Special Operations Techniques Course. This course was highly secure, difficult, intense, and stressful. It would demand all of Dan's attention. In order to relieve stress while at this school, Dan and one of his fellow Alpha Company Raider team members met on occasion at an Irish pub to play the "Big Game Hunter" video game. After several meetings at the pub, the two had erased all of the scores and replaced them with their own higher scores under the name of "A Co." One day, Dan called Tommy and told him to meet him ASAP at the pub. Tommy, not knowing what the emergency might be, hurried to meet Dan. When he arrived, he found Dan feverishly playing "Big Game Hunter," trying to restore their scoring record. For some reason, the machine had been unplugged, and all of the scores had been erased. The Marines figured it was their duty to fill the top spots with their company name once again. Apparently, the Advanced Special Operations Techniques Course didn't require all of their attention.

Dan tried to get enough sleep and still get his work done for the course. Time and stress management were a big part of the training, and Dan had become pretty good at both. He was allowed by the instructors to help out a few of the other struggling students even though the work was usually supposed to be completed independently.

One day, Dan was operating on very little sleep and trying to do several things at once. He was driving his rental car, trying to find his way on his phone's GPS, observing everything and everyone around him, and thinking ahead to what he had to do. He was great at multitasking, but this proved to be too much. Dan was driving on a road that ran parallel to the mass transit railroad route. Somehow he made a turn and ended up on the railroad track instead of on the street he needed. As he looked up from his phone, he realized where he was. Worse yet, he saw that a train was coming towards him! Dan, always cool, calm, and collected, simply slammed the rental vehicle into reverse and gunned the engine to back off the tracks. When he reported this story later in the classroom, every student and instructor was left helpless with laughter.

Dan finished the Advanced Special Operations Techniques Course with high recommendations from his instructors. He had a new set of skills and qualifications that presented different opportunities for his career. He returned home to California and spent a brief time with his wife before flying to meet his already deployed A-Co team on Camp Leatherneck in Afghanistan on May 15, 2011.

- 10 -
A DEPLOYMENT CUT SHORT

Camp Leatherneck is an international base in southern Afghanistan. It is known as Camp Bastion to the British. The objective of the Raider presence there in 2011 was to train Afghan commandos to become their own homegrown militia in order to resist the Taliban insurgency. Camp Leatherneck was a fairly modern base, located in the Helmand Province. It even boasted its own airstrip. The companies from 1st Raider Battalion rotated through and resided on the Afghan side of the base. It was the farthest point in camp from the airstrip in a somewhat unsecured area called Camp Shorbak. While some of the Raiders were busy training, planning, and preparing for missions, the others were engaging in actual missions with the commandos. The Raiders alternated between the training for and conduction of the missions.

Because of Dan's late arrival to Afghanistan, he didn't have one set role. Instead, he helped out in multiple areas. When Dan's team wasn't outside the wire participating in missions, they were busy mentoring the Afghan commandos in marksmanship and close quarter combat skills. They involved the Afghan commandos in planning and rehearsing their upcoming missions. Dan helped with some human intelligence operations their team was conducting and acted as the operations chief for his team chief.

Dan led commandos in several cordon and search missions in the Upper Helmand River Valley. In cordon and search missions, a specific target area is cordoned off and searched extensively for weapons, explosives, drugs, or any number of other illegal substances. The area might also be searched for insurgent or terrorist personnel. The missions generally lasted from 48-96 hours, but occasionally would extend a bit longer.

Camp Shorbak had its own helipad, and every mission was conducted using a raid-style insertion and extraction by either a CH-47 or CH-53 helicopter. It was often difficult to get the Afghan commandos to rappel quickly and efficiently out of the choppers on a rope into an unsafe area. Because of their hesitancy and lack of haste, they provided slow moving targets for the insurgents to shoot at. Even so, insertion by helicopter was safer than traveling to each objective in convoys which were known as IED magnets.

In late June and early July, 2011, Dan's team was engaged in a three-week operation. A permanent patrol base was being set up in the small dusty village of Puzeh. The village was located in the middle of the rugged brown hills of the Upper Helmand River Valley. Dan's team was holding security until the base could be established. It was hot in the high desert location. Thankfully, though, Puzeh was located near the Helmand River. It was not quite as uncomfortable as the rocky desert wasteland areas further from the river. Despite the gentle breeze, the flies, fleas, and mosquitoes made life miserable for the inhabitants of the small town, as well as for the Marines and Afghan commandos on the patrol base. The operation was fairly quiet. There had been a bit of IED activity and some quick harassing firefights, but nothing of major consequence.

On July 5, in the operation's second week, Dan's team was observing the southwest perimeter of Puzeh from outside the main patrol base. Their main objective was to remind the insurgents that they were still holding the town. Things had been very quiet, too quiet to please the team. Dan, being aggressive and confident in his tactical skills, decided that this was a good opportunity to find the enemy. They would take care of them before they could enter the town and sneak up on the Marine and commando positions. Dan's patrol proceeded west down a tree-lined, dirt path and entered an open poppy field at the end.

Suddenly, they came under enemy small arms fire. Dan headed toward a nearby ditch, trying to gain a better shooting position. As soon as he left the cover of the trees, Dan felt as if he had slammed his knee into a trailer hitch while running at full speed. He tried to continue, but his left leg would not sustain his weight. He fell to the ground and crawled the remainder of the way to the ditch. Thankfully, Dan was not hit with a well-aimed shot. Instead, a ricochet off the ground struck Dan's knee.

While his patrol mates continued to return fire, Dan made the radio call to the patrol base. He was so calm in giving the information identifying the wounded individual that the recipient of the call reminded him that he was supposed to give the information of the wounded man and not his own information. Dan patiently repeated the information, stating that it was himself that was down. The patrol continued to fire upon the enemy position, and Dan continued to press the fight by mentoring his Afghan commandos. Eventually, Dan was taken back to the patrol base in Puzeh. The team medics stabilized him, dressed and splinted his leg, and gave him a morphine (actually fentanyl, but the guys all called it morphine) lollipop to alleviate the pain.

Before leaving Camp Leatherneck for this particular mission, Dan had, as each one of the guys did before any mission, packed a "go bag." The bag contained civilian clothes, phone, wallet, and a few personal comfort items. It was left on his rack. The guys remaining on base could grab the go bag and get it to the wounded individual before they were transported to Germany or the States. While Dan was being transported by helicopter from the Puzeh patrol base to Camp Leatherneck, his fellow Raiders grabbed his go bag and raced to the hospital to be there when he arrived.

As soon as his Raider teammates realized that Dan wasn't dying, they began to make fun of him. They gave him some grief about arriving late for the deployment and leaving early. Then they accused him of dangling his leg out in the open in the hopes of getting a Purple Heart. After a day or two of encouragement from those guys, who provided almost constant company while he was at the hospital at Camp Leatherneck, Dan was mercifully flown to Landstuhl, Germany for higher-level care.

Dan was able to call his wife and the rest of the family several times from Afghanistan as well as from Germany. He knew that his knee was injured, but he didn't know how badly it had been damaged. He had one surgery in the hospital at Camp Leatherneck to open and clean the wound. In Germany, he had another surgery to do the same thing. Combat wounds are dirty wounds, and the risk of infection is high. Reconstructive surgery would have to wait until Dan returned to Balboa Naval Hospital in San Diego. Highly-qualified, specialist doctors would assess the damage and fix what they could.

From Germany, Dan was flown to Bethesda Naval Hospital. A few days later he was flown to San Diego. Dan didn't arrive in San Diego until over a week had passed since he had been wounded. In that time, he had traveled many hours and many miles on a gurney and been in three—now four—different hospitals. Throughout his journey, he had tried, somewhat unsuccessfully, to keep up with pain medication while under the care of constantly changing medical personnel. Besides all of that, he was returning from a combat zone to a civilian environment with no time to readjust. He was extremely impatient and not very easy to deal with.

Shortly after Dan arrived in San Diego, Karl, Rebecca, and I flew from Michigan to help him and his wife for the next couple of weeks. We were all anxious to know just how badly damaged Dan's knee was. He kept it immobilized to avoid further injury, but he was able to move around fairly well on crutches. By the time we saw him, he had the pain back under control. Dan was optimistic about his recovery. He knew that the best surgeons in the world would be doing the reconstruction. After the surgery, he would be able to work with some of the best physical therapists and the most up-to-date equipment in the world. Until the actual reconstruction surgery took place, though, nobody would know the extent of the damage or the true prognosis for recovery.

On the day before Dan's reconstructive surgery, we took him to Camp Pendleton to get acquainted with the battalion doctor and therapists who would be in charge of his rehabilitation. From there, we drove him to Balboa Naval Hospital to meet with the surgeon and get his surgery schedule. It was a long day and by the time we left Balboa, Dan was exhausted and very grumpy. The previous two weeks of travel and adjustments, the pain meds, and his wounded leg were all taking their toll. Dan would never quit, but at the moment, he was struggling to keep going.

The next day, two weeks after Dan was injured, he finally had the reconstructive surgery. The surgery took more than twice as long as anticipated. The ricochet bullet had entered Dan's knee with substantial force, completely shattering his kneecap. Had it been a direct hit, Dan would most likely have lost his leg entirely. As it was, the surgeon was able to salvage seven pieces of the shattered kneecap. He put them together with the help of wires, screws, springs, and other hardware to form what looked like a fossilized shadow of the original. The hope was that the bone fragments would knit together and heal. Hopefully, some of the hardware could be removed in a later surgery. The surgeon suggested that although Dan's injury wasn't life-threatening, it would almost certainly be life-altering. His future as a Raider operator was doubtful.

It would be interesting to compare Dan's knees after this injury had time to heal. The year before Dan had left home for recruit training, he had injured his right knee. It was a crazy injury, but much in keeping with Dan's personality. We were at a marina on the 4th of July, 2002, with another family. At supper time, we grilled hot dogs, brats, and burgers. Dan had some trouble with the relish, which was supposed to squeeze nicely out of the bottle, but was too chunky to work well. "Macho Man Dan" squeezed really hard. When the relish finally exited the bottle as a result of the extreme pressure Dan was exerting, it spewed all over his swim trunks. Dan climbed down a ladder and hopped into the water to rinse his shorts, completely ignoring the sign that said, "NO SWIMMING, JUMPING, OR DIVING!" We tried to point it out to him, but signs and rules were for people not named Dan. When he climbed back up the ladder and stood in the grass, he glanced down at his leg. We all gawked at the blood streaming from a deep gash just above his right knee. He had hopped right onto a submerged steel corrugated sea wall.

"Oh, I must have hit that on something," he said. "It will be fine with a little duct tape and maybe a rag or something." He looked at it a little closer. The guy we were with turned white and walked away. "Maybe we should have it checked out," Dan finally agreed.

In the emergency room, the gash was loosely stitched, allowing the wound to drain to prevent infection. Dan was given a prescription for a strong antibiotic since the leg was injured in water presumably filled with bacteria. He wore a leg immobilizer for a couple of weeks until the stitches healed. The gash had missed the joint capsule by mere millimeters. Dan's main concern at the time was that it would alter his intentions to enter the Marine Corps the following year. The injury didn't affect the strength or mobility of the leg after it healed, but the quad muscle remained smaller than the other leg's. We often teased Dan about his "Nemo fin." Now that Dan was wounded in the other knee, we wondered if he had just wanted that leg to match his other Nemo fin.

- 11 -
GETTING BACK IN THE FIGHT

For the first couple of weeks following Dan's surgery, he remained on heavy pain medication. He continued to suffer from the abrupt transition from the battlefield to a painful civilian existence. He was determined to push the fight and rehab as quickly as possible. Of course, he pushed harder than he should have before his knee could heal. Nobody argued with Dan, though. Two days after his reconstructive surgery, he got a ride to the gym to work out. After a few weeks, Dan decided that the pain meds were not helping his mental state. Even though they helped to control the physical pain, he quit taking them. After approximately six weeks on the opioid pain medications, he was already dependent on them. Quitting them cold turkey left him not only in physical pain but in depression for several days. Dan wanted to just sit on the couch and cry. Of course he wouldn't give in to that desire. His mental toughness helped him through it, and his new job gave him purpose and determination to keep going. The new job was to recover as quickly as possible.

Dan's team was still in Afghanistan fighting the GWOT (Global War On Terror) without him. Dan refused to sit still or feel sorry for himself for long. His goal was to get back in the fight. He had to be careful not to re-injure his knee or mess up the reconstruction that had taken place, but as soon as the initial healing took place, Dan could get started on physical therapy. This would be his main focus for the next several months. He had other duties given to him, but in his mind none were as important as his therapy and workouts in the gym.

For several weeks, Dan was dependent on other people to drive him where he had to go. He couldn't maneuver his leg into position in his wife's vehicle in order to drive safely. When he had deployed in May, he had sold his 2002 Chevy Cavalier with the intention of purchasing a pickup truck when he returned home from deployment. Now that the deployment had been cut short, he would not accrue as much money on imminent danger and separation pay as he had anticipated. He had less cash with which to buy a vehicle than he had hoped to have. The old debate about vehicles began again. This time, though, the truck won out. In September, after almost six years of talking about it, Dan finally bought a brand new 2011 Ford F-150 pickup. He now had a vehicle that would accommodate his wounded leg, and he could get around on his own. Of equal importance to his family was the fact that they would no longer have to listen to him talk about buying a truck.

Day after day at the battalion headquarters, Dan worked with the physical therapists. He pushed himself harder than anyone else. The therapists had to hold him back so that he didn't do any damage to his reconstructed knee. He worked to increase strength in his leg. That was easy. Increasing its range of motion was more difficult and more painful. Dan worked his two therapists against each other. If one could get the knee to bend fifteen degrees one day, Dan would say to the other one on the next day, "Only fifteen degrees? We got more than that yesterday." The therapist would then work it a little harder and maybe get another degree or two. Dan would sweat and squirm and use a little more ice when the session was over. He iced it regularly and tried to keep it elevated at night to keep the swelling down. He would not back off on his workouts, no matter how much it hurt.

Although Dan's therapy and workouts occupied much of his time, he was also given the responsibility of scheduling Special Activities Training for the battalion. Dan had a lot of experience in this area beginning back in high school. He had always been the one who had a plan, knew the plan, or was making a plan. He was a whirlwind of activity, and even while competently handling things at work, could be talking on his phone and making plans for Friday night. He was fun and creative and would always communicate with everyone so that nobody was left out.

The billet of Special Activities Training coordinator was a little more challenging than that of social coordinator for a group of high school friends. It was usually filled by a higher ranking non-commissioned officer than Dan's current rank of staff sergeant, but as a result of his injury, Dan needed a job that required minimal physical activity. He had been selected for promotion to gunnery sergeant and hoped to pick that up within a year. Besides, he had proven himself to be capable of handling billets in the past that were above his rank and experience level. He handled this job so well that the battalion begged him to stay in that position. But Dan was already looking ahead to his next deployment.

Dan's responsibility as Special Activities Training Coordinator was to schedule and coordinate training schools and activities for all of the 1st Raider Battalion Marines. It was his responsibility to insure that each Marine attending a particular school had completed the necessary prerequisites and had the proper equipment for each school. He went over gear lists and battalion expectations with the men who would be attending various schools. It was a very demanding job that required a lot of phone and email communication with the guys and with the various schools they would be attending. For some, the job would be considered high stress. Dan thrived in high stress situations.

Dan's days of physical therapy, workouts, and activity coordination were long and full. Dan was asked to drive to Phoenix, Arizona, in November to be the lead facilitator in Alpha Company's "Third Location Decompression" when they arrived home from Afghanistan. He jumped at the opportunity. Not only would it be a break from his hectic routine, but it would give him the opportunity to welcome "his guys" home from deployment. He would be able to help them make a seamless transition back to civilian life. His main responsibility in Phoenix would be to drive the Marines around and keep them out of trouble for a few days while they reintegrated into civilian life. He was eager to see the guys and show them how much he had recovered from what should have been a career-ending injury. Dan drove a large passenger van from California to Arizona. He carried his teammates around Phoenix for several days in much the same manner as he had escorted his recon team a few years earlier. Then he had been too young to legally drink and by default was their designated driver. Now, he was put in charge of their safekeeping by the 1st Raider Battalion command.

Dan returned to California after the "Third Location Decompression" and spent the next month continuing his rehabilitation. He had an opportunity to fill an opening on a deployment the following spring if he could get reinstated to full duty. In order for that to happen, he had to be cleared by the battalion doctor, and he had to pass a physical fitness test. There were several reasons for his hurry to deploy. It was in his nature to want to be whole and healthy and qualified to do his job. He wanted his job to be a Raider operator. Because of his shortened deployment, he didn't have the cash to buy his truck. He had hated to take out a loan, but he needed a vehicle right away. Dan's current enlistment was ending soon. He wouldn't be allowed to reenlist if he couldn't get cleared for full duty and pass his physical. He wanted to reenlist while he was deployed because his bonus would be maximized with out-of-country benefits. The push was on, and Dan was up to the task.

• • •

In December of 2011, Dan and his wife flew to Michigan for another visit. Friends and family had followed Dan's progress after he was wounded and were eager to see him. Dan was always eager to spend time at home where he had grown up. During the holidays, Dan was able to visit with many friends and family members. After one visit with my parents, Dan commented that it might very well be the last time that he would see them alive. Again, he noticed them weakening with age. He spent time with Rebecca's husband, shooting guns and talking about guns and ammunition. Although he continued to share a special bond with Rebecca, Dan seemed content to give up the protection of his little sister to her husband.

Dan wondered how his wounded knee would react to the cold Michigan winter. It became evident that there was already some arthritis in it. He had to work hard just to keep the stiffness and soreness at bay. He continued with therapy and workouts while he was home and managed to maintain the strength and flexibility he had achieved. He wasn't able to make much progress, though, and he decided that he would never be comfortable living in an area with cold winters. For now, he still had his eye on the deployment deadline, and the physical fitness deadline that came with it.

After Christmas, Karl and I drove Dan and his wife back to California. It was a wonderful three-and-a-half day trip. Karl was the primary driver, and I was the chief navigator. Dan did some driving and was the "food police." He determined when and where we would eat. Since Karl and I were paying the way as a Christmas gift to Dan and his wife, Dan was very cost conscious. He worked hard, with his great negotiating skills, to make every meal a pleasant experience. Dan's wife was put in charge of their little dog who traveled with us.

After we arrived in California, we stayed ten days with Dan and his wife in their San Marcos home. While we were there, Dan planned a lot of hiking activities that would further his rehab as well as test the strength of his injured leg. First, though, he decided that my hiking boots had to be replaced. I had purchased them over thirty years before while in college.

We all piled into "Jasper," Dan's new pickup truck, and made a trip to the REI store in San Diego. Dan helped me pick out a nice pair of Merrell boots that were sturdy, comfortable, and felt broken in immediately. Now we were ready.

The first hike that Dan planned was at Mission Trails Regional Park. It was a very warm, sunny day, and the rocky, red clay trail rose and fell steeply. We weren't very prepared for the hot, dry, difficult hike and we all struggled to have fun with it. Dan's leg was hurting by the time we returned to Jasper in the parking lot, and since we had taken no water along, we were very hot and thirsty. It wasn't a great first hike, but it was a start, and we all enjoyed the time we spent together.

After a day or two, Dan was ready to go again. This time he chose Mount Woodson. We left for the excursion shortly after the sun rose, knowing that the day would heat up quickly. After a thirty-minute drive, Dan drove Jasper into the parking area at the Poway Reservoir Recreation Area. He confidently pulled into a handicap parking space, explaining as he did so that his temporary handicap parking pass would expire soon and he had to make use of it while he could. It seemed a little silly to be using the handicap space to save walking a few feet in the parking lot to begin a nine mile hike, but as Dan hung the pass on Jasper's rearview mirror, he explained with his big, silly grin that he didn't know how he would feel after the hike. He wanted to be parked as close as possible.

We started off around the Poway Reservoir much more prepared than we had been at Mission Trails. We took water and snacks and planned for a 4-5 hour hike. The climb up Mount Woodson was rugged, steep, rocky, and beautiful. The sun was hot, and the clear air allowed terrific views of northern San Diego County out to the Pacific Ocean. Near the top of Mount Woodson, we encountered a popular medium-difficulty rock climbing area. Dan wanted to do some climbing, but decided that he would have to wait for another time when his leg was completely healed. For that day, it was enough to climb to the summit and enjoy the view. After snacking and resting we started the descent, which caused Dan more pain than the ascent. Even though he was sore and tired when we reached the bottom, he wouldn't take the easy way out. After making sure that his "aging" parents were up to it, he decided to take the longer trail around the reservoir to get back to Jasper who waited in his handicap parking space.

The final hiking trip Dan planned was to Palomar Mountain State Park. In contrast to the weather on our day at Mount Woodson, the day at Palomar Mountain was cold, snowy, sleety, and miserable. Dan's knee complained again about the cold, wet weather, and we did very little hiking. Instead, we explored the observatory and drove around on some of the less traveled vehicle paths in the park. It was a good day, in spite of the evidence that Dan's knee was far from 100% and probably would never be without pain.

On the days we didn't hike, Dan didn't sit still and rest. He and Karl worked on several yard and garden, maintenance, and construction projects on those days. Dan had a way of making work and play equally tiring and fun. The work days proved to test Dan's rehabbing leg just as much as the hiking days did. Although Dan's wife couldn't join us for most of our activities because of her work, she was able to accompany us to the San Diego Zoo Wild Animal Park. That was the one relaxing day that Dan allowed himself during this holiday leave. It still involved a substantial amount of walking.

• • •

Dan continued to push himself and work his therapists against each other in order to be ready to deploy in April. He assured his commanding officer that he would make it. The battalion doctor commented that she wished all of her patients worked as hard as the wounded Raiders did. They pushed themselves harder than anyone else. The main job of their therapists was to keep them from re-injuring themselves. Finally, in early April of 2012, just nine months after sustaining what probably should have been a debilitating, career-changing injury, Dan achieved an almost perfect score on a physical fitness test and was reinstated to full active duty.

On April 23, twenty-six-year-old Staff Sergeant Daniel J. Price deployed with Special Operations Task Force West to Camp Lawton in Herat, Afghanistan. The SOTF, as it was called, was responsible to oversee all US Special Operations Forces combat operations within the Helmand River Valley. The Helmand River Valley covered more than a thousand square miles of high desert and mountainous terrain. Even though Dan was the junior operations officer in the SOTF office, he kept busy helping with mission planning for the Marine Special Operations teams and analyzing after-mission reports. The SOTF assisted the teams in their endeavors to train and encourage the Afghan commando forces to establish their own counter insurgency force. Just as he had before on many occasions, Dan now exceeded his rank and experience level in his job performance. The advanced training he had received at the Advanced Special Operations Course in the spring of 2011 had qualified him for his duties with the SOTF. His combat experience gave him valuable insight into combat operations and mission planning. On a couple of occasions, Dan even had the opportunity to help NATO special operations forces capture international terrorists in and around the city of Herat.

Dan reenlisted as soon as possible after arriving in Afghanistan. With his reenlistment bonus, he made arrangements to pay off his truck. On June 9, 2012, the day after turning twenty-seven years old and just short of nine years in the Marine Corps, Dan was promoted to gunnery sergeant. His career seemed to be on track. He was successful as an operator and in whatever leadership positions he was placed. Other than a few trips in support of teams on FOBs, it seemed that this deployment would present minimal combat danger.

Needing to stay busy at all times, Dan helped out with various maintenance projects around the base and on vehicles and equipment. In addition to his required duties, he worked out regularly in the gym to stay in shape and to increase strength and range of motion in his recovering knee. Dan added a lot of fun to the SOTF, as well. One of the big projects he engineered in his spare time was the construction of a huge barbecue grill with a lid that was raised and lowered by hydraulic power. It was the talk of Camp Lawton and all of the guys greatly enjoyed using it to grill whatever they could find. The guys Dan worked with in the SOTF office loved giving him a hard time, and he humored them by responding with equal banter.

Although Dan cheerfully and efficiently did his job with the SOTF, he really wanted to be operating with a team on combat missions. He hung out with the Raider teams on Camp Lawton whenever he could. He continuously positioned himself to deliver equipment and information to teams on FOBs and in the field. In the year since Dan had been wounded, he had wanted desperately to get back in the fight.

On his second deployment to Iraq in 2005, Dan had experienced similar frustration when his commanding officer had forced him out of the fight by insisting that he come in from the field to compete in a board interview for a meritorious promotion. At that time, his commander told him that he could come in kicking and screaming, or he could come willingly. Either way, he was coming in from the field and doing the board exam. Dan submitted and diligently prepared. He did such a fine job during the examination that the officers on the board questioned whether his wrong answers were actually correct. His skill in debate came as no surprise. Even while growing up, Dan tenaciously argued any point at all, just for the sake of proving his position. It didn't really matter whether he was right or wrong. He passed the meritorious board exam and was promoted to sergeant. He had been in the Marine Corps for just over two years. The promotion wasn't important to Dan. Getting back to his team was what mattered then, and it was his goal now.

One of the companies from 2nd Marine Raider Battalion was deployed to Camp Lawton. Their home base was Camp Lejeune, North Carolina. Even though Dan's home base was Camp Pendleton, California, he knew many of the guys from training and hanging out with them while being in Afghanistan. The teams from 2nd Raider Battalion were getting hammered pretty heavily that summer. They had sustained several casualties, with some being wounded and others being killed in action. The team was short-handed. Dan was finally given permission to join Team 8232 to help direct the Afghan commandos in a mission to secure a compound in the Helmand River Valley in Baghdis Province. The mission was to take place on July 29, 2012.

- 12 -
THE END...AND THE BEGINNING

At 2:45 on Sunday afternoon, July 29, 2012, the front doorbell of our home rang. We don't have a walk leading to our front door, and nobody ever goes through the grass to get there, so I told Karl to see who was there. We had been resting in the family room at the back of the house. As Karl rounded the corner on his way to the front door, he said that I had better come. His tone of voice did not bode well. As I followed him into the living room and came into view of the door, I saw three Marines in Alpha uniforms standing outside on the doorstep. Karl and I both knew. We didn't need to hear the words that followed. "Are you Daniel Price's father?" When Karl affirmed that he was, we were asked to sit down.

When we had been seated, one of the Marines stated, "On behalf of the President of the United States of America and the Commandant of the United States Marine Corps, I regret to inform you that Gunnery Sergeant Daniel Joseph Price was killed this morning in combat operations in Afghanistan." Simultaneously, in California, Dan's wife received the identical message from members of Dan's 1st Raider Battalion Alpha Company. In a split second, our lives changed forever.

How did it happen? The details were pretty vague and not very accurate, as we would later discover. Something was said about small arms fire and a head wound. We immediately jumped to the conclusion that there could be things worse than death. But, Dan was so good at what he did! "So was Charlie," Dan had often said regarding one of his good friends who had been killed in 2009.

But, how could it happen? From 2001 through 2012, there had been just over 2,000 troops killed in Afghanistan. In 2012, only about 300 were killed. The casualty numbers were much higher in other conflicts. On D-Day alone, the estimated death toll of US troops ranges from 2,500–5,000. Almost 417,000 US troops lost their lives in the entirety of WWII. The Afghanistan numbers pale in comparison and seem insignificant—until one is your son. The numbers are never again insignificant. Each subsequent KIA hurts in a very personal way.

Suddenly, the remote possibility was a reality. It no longer mattered that he was one of the best, fighting alongside of the best. His extensive training meant nothing. His sniper qualifications became worthless. It seemed like such a waste. What is the purpose of such deep emotional pain manifested so intensely that we experienced physical pain in our bodies?

The Marines in our living room offered to accompany us to inform other relatives or to assist in any way. Karl and I decided that we should do it alone. For the next several hours we made our visits. First, Rebecca. Then our pastor, who would make the announcement at the evening worship service. Next, our other son, followed by Dan's grandparents. As we drove from house to house, I asked the question, "What will God accomplish in this, and how will he be glorified?" While I was numb with shock and grief, God filled me with an excitement about what He would accomplish. It was an excitement that was surreal. I immediately hoped for a renewed relationship with our other son, and his family. That relationship had deteriorated over the past several years. I hoped that in taking one son from us, God might restore the other to us. As I write this almost six years later, we continue to pray for that restoration, as we patiently wait for God's answer.

When we finally returned home after making the announcement, our pastor had arrived at our house. Matt and Rebecca came to be with us. Rebecca was five months pregnant and devastated by the news of Dan's death. She had lulled herself into a false sense of security because Dan had been deployed on a non-combat deployment with the SOTF. Our pastor warned us to give some thought to how we would handle the media, as it was sure to show up. We should decide ahead of time whether we would grant interviews, and if so, what we should say. He read scripture and had prayer, then left us with friends and family members to try to process our feelings.

As we began our painful journey, we were comforted to see evidences of God's care for us. On the day before Dan's death, we had returned home from a week-long youth convention. The theme had been "Soar Like Eagles," and the theme verse was taken from Isaiah 40:31: "Those who hope in the Lord will renew their strength. They will soar on wings like eagles. They will run and not grow weary, they will walk and not be faint." God had been strengthening and encouraging us for a journey we hadn't known we would take. We were privileged to meet and talk to Pastor Vos at the convention. He had been Dan's pastor at Escondido United Reformed Church, but had moved a year earlier to pastor a church in Michigan just ten miles from where we live. In God's providence, He allowed us to establish a relationship with Pastor Vos, who would only two weeks later conduct Dan's funeral in Holland, Michigan.

As a result of us having been gone to attend the convention, our dog was at the home of our friends who took care of her whenever we were away from home. It hadn't worked out to bring the dog back home on Saturday. On Monday morning, I called our friend and told her that Dan had been killed. She immediately agreed to keep the dog until further notice. They had the dog at their house for over two months. It was a tiny detail that God took care of. It was a great relief not to think about our dog when our minds were barely able to function. We were so thankful that the dog was not around in the following days and weeks as we traveled to Dover, entertained friends, family, and strangers, participated in visitation and funeral events, and traveled to California for memorial events there.

At five o'clock in the evening of July 30, the Department of Defense released the information of Dan's death to the media. At five o'clock in the evening of July 30, two local television stations pulled up in front of our house and asked for interviews. Karl and I had agreed that we were called to use the circumstances that God placed us in to be faithful to Him, to spread His gospel message as well as we could, and to bring glory to His name.

The reporters who came were friendly and compassionate. They made the interview very comfortable. We conveyed a message of confidence in God's plan. We made it known that although others saw Dan as a hero, a term he scoffed at, he was just a home-grown farm kid who loved his family, his country, and most importantly, his God. His faith gave him the courage and the drive to succeed.

Many people from around the country and world reacted to the interview. We received one letter from an old lady that we did not know. The letter said:

In watching TV last eve—you two were there. I was so very saddened to hear of the tragic passing of your boy. At my age (87) I've had to say my 'Good-byes' to most of my family—tough, but to lose a child, I've never had to encounter. I can't even fathom the pain, but your words concerning your and your son's faith in God—wow, you'll never know the lives you've touched by your doing and...you made our God happy.

Angry tension filled a conference room at Camp Lawton in Herat, Afghanistan. The Marines there had lost two of their brothers—two of the best. They were so angry, they were ready to shoot the laundry guy, simply because he was an Afghan. One of the wives sent a link to our televised interview. It was shown on the large screen in the conference room. God used the showing of that interview to melt the anger and animosity of the men in the room. As the eighty-seven-year-old woman had written, we would "never know the lives that would be touched" by our interview.

On Tuesday, our assigned CACO (Casualty Assistance Call Officer) picked us up around noon to fly to Philadelphia to witness the dignified transfer of Dan's body to the mortuary at Dover Air Force Base. The CACO had been among the three who came to our home on Sunday. He was assigned to assist us in any way he could for as long as he was needed. He arranged for all of our travel to Philadelphia and from there, to Dover Air Force Base, where Dan's body would arrive from Afghanistan.

This was the fourth time that I would be flying. The first time, I had flown to San Diego for Dan's recruit training graduation. The second time, I flew into Los Angeles with John's mom to visit the boys before Dan's second deployment to Iraq. My third time flying was into Los Angeles with Karl for Dan's Scout Sniper graduation. Now my fourth time to fly was to witness the return of Dan's body to the United States from Afghanistan. Although each of my flight experiences had something to do with Dan's military career, it was with very different emotions that we boarded this flight. I couldn't help but cry during most of the flight. It was still connected with Dan's military career, but I was not filled with eager anticipation or celebration. I was overwhelmed with crushing grief.

After landing in Philadelphia, we boarded a rental vehicle shuttle. Another group of people sat down across from us on the shuttle. Karl received a phone call from an elder in our church and explained where we were and where we were heading. When he finished the call, the young man across the aisle on the rental car shuttle asked who he was. Karl told him, and the young man introduced himself and said, "My brother was killed with your son." They came from Florida, we from Michigan. It amazed us that we all arrived at the airport at the same time and ended up on the same rental shuttle. We were all going to Dover to observe the dignified transfer of our loved ones' bodies from the cargo plane to the van transporting them to the mortuary. Only God could organize and arrange for that timing in the busy transportation world.

Before we left the rental car agency, Dan's wife arrived with her mom, her friend who was John's wife, and her CACO. We spent the next two days together at the Fisher House on Dover Air Force Base. The Fisher House was warm and accommodating, providing food and a comfortable place to stay while waiting for the bodies to return and the dignified transfer to take place. Since our minds were numb and unthinking, it was good to be taken where we needed to be and told what would take place at each step of the way.

On Wednesday morning, the plane carrying the two bodies arrived in Dover. There were multiple thunderstorms and threats of tornadoes in the area. We had often referred to Dan as our family's tornado, and it was just a bit ironic that the return of his body was accompanied by such tumultuous weather.

When we saw the containers that carried the bodies being transported from the airplane to the transport van, I had two thoughts. The first was that the container was way too small to hold Dan's huge personality. The second that followed immediately, was the fact that Dan was no longer with his body. It was an emotional moment of recognition that Dan was truly gone from us. We would never see him again, never hear his laugh, and never again hear his voice.

Dan's friend, John, was deployed to Afghanistan at the time of Dan's death. He was able to escort Dan's body back to the states. What a blessing that was. We were good friends with John, his wife, and his parents. John's parents had come to our house on the evening of Dan's death to comfort us and to be comforted. The relationships that had been built up over the past eight years were another evidence of God's goodness to us. The time we had spent with John's parents had fostered an open and comfortable relationship that God used, and continues to use, to sustain and comfort us.

We were eager to talk with John when he arrived with Dan's body. We realized that he was in the middle of perhaps his most difficult mission ever. He not only had to escort one of his best friends back in a box, he also had to minister to the family who had become friends over the years. John was trained to maintain his composure in difficult circumstances and to get the job done. He carried out his duties flawlessly. The escorts had a little trouble in Germany when an Air Force kid wasn't going to allow them to accompany the bodies to a storage area. They eventually worked it out and were able to remain with the bodies the entire way from Afghanistan to Dover. John remained in Dover until Dan's body was released for transport to Holland, Michigan, when he escorted it on the final leg of Dan's journey from Afghanistan.

The days following our return home from Dover were strange. We were busy, but spent a lot of time waiting. We waited a week for the Dover mortuary to release Dan's body to be transported to Michigan. Dan's wife along with her CACO made all of the funeral arrangements, so we weren't busy with that. They had to wait to complete the arrangements until we knew when the body would arrive. We kept busy with family, friends, and Marines who came to visit.

In 2009, when Dan told us about the combat incident in Shewan for which he received the Bronze Star Medal, I asked him how he made it out of there alive, much less uninjured. He replied, "I guess my work isn't finished, yet." One of the Marines who visited us in the week after Dan was killed, told us that he was part of that unfinished work. In 2011, that Marine had gone to the Advanced Special Operations Techniques Course with Dan. He was the one who had established A-Co's reputation on "Big Game Hunter" with Dan. They had deployed together in 2011, and he was with Dan when he had been wounded. Dan's influence on him had helped him grow in his relationship with God. He told us that he had become a stronger, better Christian because of Dan. We appreciated knowing of Dan's witness to a fellow Marine.

Another Marine told us that even though Dan had been younger with less rank and less experience in the Marine Corps, they all looked up to him. He said, "We all wanted to be Dan." This Marine gave his third child, born four years after Dan's death, the middle name of "Price" in honor of Dan.

Each Marine who came to our house and wandered around our property and in the barns remarked how they felt as though they had been here before. Everything was just as Dan had described it so often to them. Knowing how fondly Dan had talked of home to his teammates was another way that God comforted us in those early days. The Marines thanked us for the upbringing that had helped make Dan the man he had been.

On August 8, Dan's body was scheduled to arrive in Holland. Early in the morning, we noticed several military helicopters flying overhead. The security was tight. We didn't know why, but guessed maybe because of the presence of the special operatives or because of the state and local government officials in attendance. We had invited family and close friends to be present at the airport when Dan's body arrived. At ten that morning, ten days after Dan was killed, the jet carrying his body landed at the West Michigan Regional Airport. It didn't take long to transfer the casket to the waiting hearse and make the short trip from the airport to the funeral home. The procession route was lined with people waving flags and giving somber salutes as we passed.

After the body was brought into the funeral home, Karl said a brief prayer, and the family members and friends dispersed. Several people commented on the beauty of Karl's prayer. Neither he nor I could remember what he said in the prayer, but we trusted the words of Romans 8:26 which say, "Likewise the Spirit also helps in our weaknesses. For we do not know what we should pray for as we ought, but the Spirit Himself makes intercession for us with groanings which cannot be uttered." The prayer of comfort and encouragement came from the Holy Spirit.

We went out for lunch with several Marines and family members. While we were eating, the owner of the restaurant came in. When she heard that we were there, she told the staff that there was no charge for our lunch. After lunch, our family returned to the funeral home.

While we had been gone, the funeral director prepared Dan's body for viewing. Dan's wife insisted that we view the body. At the time, I didn't think it was important. In the years since, I have been grateful for her insight. It is important that we saw the body and know that it was Dan. Occasionally, because of the high security and sensitivity of Dan's job, a nagging thought comes into my mind that his death may have been staged so that he could engage in unknown black ops. I find comfort in the fact that we saw Dan's body in the casket. We saw the casket placed in the ground. I am confident that Dan would never put his family through what we have experienced unnecessarily.

Visitation was scheduled for the evening of Wednesday, August 8, from five until eight, and again on Thursday, August 9, from one until four in the afternoon, and six until nine in the evening. The funeral director advised against that much visitation time, but there was a steady stream of visitors and a lengthy wait for some during the sessions. The guest book was signed by well over a thousand relatives, friends, neighbors, Patriot Guard Riders, Gold Star family members, military family members, retired military personnel, and even some residents from the community who were completely unknown to the family. Members of Dan's Alpha Company team rotated positions at the head and foot of the casket during all of the visitation hours. Others mingled with and talked with the visitors. One of them was always near the family to assist in whatever way they could. Friends from church remained near, as did John's parents. A flag line outside of the funeral home was staffed by patriots and supporters, mostly unknown to us. God used each one of these people to give us strength and encouragement.

Prior to the many hours of visitation, Pastor Vos gave these words of encouragement to us from II Corinthians 1:3-7:

Blessed be the God and Father of our Lord Jesus Christ, the Father of mercies and God of all comfort, who comforts us in all our tribulation, that we may be able to comfort those who are in any trouble, with the comfort with which we ourselves are comforted by God. For as the sufferings of Christ abound in us, so our consolation also abounds through Christ. Now if we are afflicted, it is for your consolation and salvation, which is effective for enduring the same sufferings which we also suffer. Or if we are comforted, it is for your consolation and salvation. And our hope for you is steadfast, because we know that as you are partakers of the sufferings, so also you will partake of the consolation.

The strength with which we received the visitors at the funeral home can be attributed only to God's grace in and through us. God continues to give us opportunities to encourage others with the comfort which we have received from Him.

• • •

In April of 2006, we had observed another family in our community go through the loss of their son in Iraq. The death of Rick Herrema hit us pretty hard. Dan had just returned from his second deployment to Iraq as a Recon Marine. Rick was on his first deployment with Delta Force, after having served seven years in the military. He was killed by a sniper bullet while inserting by helicopter for one of his first missions.

Rick had shown 4-H livestock with our kids at the Hudsonville Community Fair, and we were acquainted with his family. Like Dan, Rick had been a highly motivated and driven individual who strove for excellence in all that he did. Rick loved God and his family, and had been brought up much like Dan. He grew up on a small hobby farm in a Christian community a few miles from our hobby farm. He had attended Christian schools and was a member of a Christian Reformed Church. Unlike Dan, Rick had enlisted in the army on a whim. It turned out to be just what he needed to give him purpose and direction. Rick soon became part of the Army Special Operations Command and trained to be a medic. He enrolled in every school he could, many of them the same or similar to the ones that Dan attended. Rick was a hero who was loved by everyone who knew him. He was an overachiever whose work ethic far exceeded the "normal range." He was described at his funeral as a man who always returned something borrowed in better condition than he had received it. The similarities between Dan and Rick were many.

When we went to the funeral home visitation and saw Rick's family after his death, we marveled at their composure. We observed their strength and apparent peace, in spite of their brokenness. We didn't understand. Now, six years later, we experienced the same peace and strength. We were broken, but God gave us the strength we needed to comfort those who came to comfort us. Our message to each visitor at the time of Dan's death was taken from Psalm 18:30, "As for God, His way is perfect."

• • •

On the day before Dan's funeral, on the base in Afghanistan where John's team was operating, an Afghan in a commando uniform opened fire in the office and killed three of John's teammates. These three were well-known to the men on Dan's team who were in attendance and acting as pallbearers at Dan's funeral. Had John not been escorting Dan's body from Afghanistan to Holland, he would have been in the office with the Marines who were killed. John's mom credited Dan with indirectly saving John's life at the time. God gave us the grace to give thanks for the fact that we didn't have to worry about Dan's deployments any longer. We didn't have to send him back into combat when he left home. His work was finished. We knew that he was truly home where nothing could harm him again.

August 11, 2012, the day of Dan's funeral, dawned bright and comfortably cool. Dan's Marine teammates escorted us to the church where the funeral would be held. Before we even reached the church property, we could see people with flags lining the street and driveways leading into the church parking lots. The parking areas were filling with cars and motorcycles hours before the funeral was scheduled to begin. Our Marine escort, using one of Dan's favorite sayings, drawled, "Now that's what right looks like!" We and the Marines were overwhelmed by the community support. The crowd included people who had driven for five or six hours to be part of a "human shield" to protect our family from any protesters.

The funeral was a beautiful celebration and remembrance of Dan's life. One of the Marines put together a slide presentation that was presented before the funeral began. Dan's wife spoke of Dan's humility, work ethic, humor, and his intense pride in fighting the GWOT, the Global War On Terror. As several of Dan's teammates spoke, we realized that we didn't know the magnitude of who he was. He told us so many things in such an understated way that it never seemed like a big deal. The Marines were hurting. Their love and respect for Dan was obvious. We continue to be surprised at the level of respect for Dan that emanates from everyone who knew him.

Several themes that continually come up with regard to Dan were spoken of by the Marines at his funeral:

- Thanks to us, Dan's parents, for raising Dan to be the man he was
- Thanks for Dan's wife for her support of everything Dan did
- Dan's extreme work ethic
- Dan's ability to endear himself to everyone he met
- Dan's equanimity, the ability to remain calm in every situation
- Dan's team chief told how Dan, "Never complained about anything, except bad guys. And he did a pretty good job of making them go away!" He also reported that Dan had saved his life on at least two occasions, and probably more.
- Another Marine said, "You don't think that the loss of one man can make a big difference, but the battalion, MARSOC, the Marine Corps is weaker today because Dan is no longer with it."

- Another stated, "Not only in his own unit, but guys in other units knew that Dan Price was a Christian. He had a pure, clean reputation."

- "On any deployment Dan would sleep with two things on his pillow: a gun, naturally, and his Bible with passages marked by pictures of his family."

- "Dan was never afraid. He always knew where he would be, if he was killed, and he was confident that he was doing the right thing."

Pastor Vos focused on Dan's primary calling as a Christian, with his secondary calling as a US Marine. As Christians, we are always on deployment in the battle against evil. Pastor Vos challenged and encouraged us with words from II Timothy 4:7-8: "I have fought the good fight; I have finished the race; I have kept the faith. Finally, there is laid up for me the crown of righteousness, which the Lord, the righteous Judge, will give to me on that Day, and not to me only but also to all who have loved His appearing."

As we exited the church after Dan's funeral, we were met with the sound of Holland's American Legion Band playing patriotic hymns. Over 1,500 Patriot Guard Riders and other motorcyclists led the funeral procession through closed, flag-lined streets to the cemetery. Many people showed their respect as the hearse passed by, carrying Dan's body to its resting place in the cemetery. The cemetery roads were lined with people, motorcycles, flags, and cars. After the funeral, one police officer was reported as saying, "With so much community support and so many people present, the protesters must have decided that it would be better not to show themselves." It was an amazing display of support and respect from a community that continues in patriotism and compassion each year when we walk through the Holland Memorial Day Parade.

After the religious committal service, Dan was honored with full military honors, including a twenty-one gun salute. The casket flag was folded and presented to Dan's wife. A second flag was presented to Karl and me. Dan's teammates, commanders, and any veterans present began paying their final respects. Each Marine Raider took their jump wings and dive bubbles off their uniforms and placed them, one by one, on Dan's casket. After a long line of military personnel paid their respects, the retired Commanding General of Marine Corps Forces Special Operations Command took his Two-Star General Officer rank insignia from the shoulder of his uniform and placed it on the casket. That was the only time that the Marines present had ever seen a general do that in honor of a fallen Marine. Dan truly held a special place in the Marine Raider community. Finally, after all of the military respects had been paid, Dan's wife and I each laid a rose on the casket and the cemetery personnel lowered it into the ground. The Marines removed their covers (hats) and gave a final tribute to Dan with "twenty-five and five" pushups completed around his open grave.

After Dan's funeral, the commanding officer of Alpha Company told us that Dan went into every combat situation with a courage unlike any other he had ever seen. Dan wasn't afraid. He knew he would not be killed before God's appointed time. He was confident of where he was going if, and when, he would be killed. He was never careless or haphazard in mission planning, but personal safety was secondary to accomplishing the mission as efficiently as possible. He also stated that Dan was the best Marine he had seen in all of his years in the Marine Corps.

One more amazing manifestation of God's perfect plan took place in the events surrounding Dan's funeral. Holland's Marine Corps League had offered to help in whatever way they could. Dan's widow had asked if they would provide a post-funeral luncheon for Dan's immediate family, out of town friends, and the Marines. They graciously agreed, and after the reception, we thanked the Marine veteran who planned it. He told us this story. The Marine Corps League of Holland had never held a fundraiser. For some reason, the previous summer, they had decided to do some sort of fundraiser. They had raised $800 and had no idea what they would do with that money. It was still waiting to be used for any need that came up. With incredulity, this member of the Marine Corps League told us that when the bills for Dan's post-funeral reception were tallied, the total came to $800. What an incredible witness of God providing for the needs of His people! He works through ordinary means and ordinary people to accomplish His purposes each and every day.

On the second anniversary of Dan's death, we were the recipients of the Silver Star Medal in honor of Dan's action on July 29, 2012 in Baghdis, Afghanistan. The Silver Star Medal is the third highest military combat award that can be earned. Once again, the community of Holland showed their support as almost 500 people attended the twenty minute presentation ceremony. One of Dan's former teammates drove sixteen hours from Camp

Lejeune to attend the ceremony. He spent about two hours in Holland, then turned around to make the return trip to North Carolina. He had begged his superiors to be allowed to make the trip. He had to be back to his teaching billet at the Raider schoolhouse as soon as possible. In spite of that, he was determined to honor Dan with his presence at that ceremony if there was any possibility of doing so. What a testimony to the love and respect that he had for Dan!

- 13 -
THE CONCLUSION OF THE MATTER

I remember telling another mom when Dan quite small, that I didn't know what God had planned for Dan. Because of his temperament, strong will, work ethic, and leadership qualities, I knew it would be something special. Dan was not an ordinary child, and by God's grace, he grew up to be an extraordinary adult. We are thankful for the privilege of parenting him for twenty-seven years. All of the obsessive/compulsive characteristics that he displayed, all of his fussiness in every detail, and all of the events of his childhood culminated in the Marine Raider, the ultimate warrior that he became.

As Dan entered his Marine Corps training, I likened his success and excellence to Joseph in the Old Testament book of Genesis. God enabled Joseph and gave him success in everything he put his hand to in order to save the Israelites, God's chosen people, from famine. They were preserved so that centuries later, Jesus could be born to be the Savior of God's children. We are thankful for the nine years that Dan served in the Marine Corps. During those years, he matured as a person, as the head of his family, and as a soldier in God's army. We are thankful for the assurance that we have of Dan's salvation in Jesus Christ. Without God, Dan was nothing. Any success he had was from God to be used for the good of God's Kingdom. As much as Dan seemed to be in control of every situation, his confidence came from knowing God controls all things.

So many things in the life of Dan have obviously been God's plan for him. I think back on Dan's childhood and see how God used his personality, his work, his play, his 4-H experiences, and everything else in his childhood to prepare him for the job he was called to do. God used and prepared us for every part we were called to do in raising Dan and letting him go when he reached adulthood. Everything in each one of our lives can be attributed to God's plan. Even when we don't recognize our circumstances as being from God, they still are part of His perfect eternal plan. We are blessed when we recognize and acknowledge God's sovereignty over every little thing that happens day by day.

God used the accident when Dan and his wife rolled their vehicle off the interstate in remote Utah, to fill me with a confidence that He was in control whether Dan was at home, in California, at a training facility, or in a combat zone in Iraq or Afghanistan. There are no stray bullets. Each one has a specific destination and a predetermined time of arrival. I repeated the phrase often and believed it wholeheartedly while Dan was deployed so many times. We had given thanks for its truth on many occasions. The bullets that claimed the life of Gunnery Sergeant Daniel Joseph Price were planned and meant for him long before he was born. We hadn't known how Dan's life would end, but God knew. He orchestrated and planned every detail for His glory and for our comfort. Can we continue to thank God in the middle of the circumstances He gave us? Without the assurance of God's sovereign providence in every circumstance, there is no hope, no purpose to continue on in the murky darkness of life.

The only purpose and value for our lives on earth comes from our relationship with God and the way in which He uses our lives in His eternal plan. This belief gives us comfort, purpose, and strength to face each new day. We are still broken, and on some days, unable to function. But God continues to rebuild us. In II Corinthians 12:9, the Apostle Paul says, "And He said to me, 'My grace is sufficient for you, for my strength is made perfect in weakness.' Therefore most gladly I will rather boast in my infirmities, that the power of Christ may rest upon me." How can we harbor bitterness or anger toward God, who uses every circumstance of life to draw His people to Himself and be glorified by it? Our prayer remains that we will be faithful to God and be used by Him to accomplish His purposes. No matter how hard the road is for us, we know that God will equip us to do whatever He calls us to. His grace has been, and will be, sufficient for us.

We miss Dan every day, but as long as we are alive on earth, we know that our work is not yet finished. God gives us opportunities to meet people from many different backgrounds. Some wish to honor Dan in some way, some have lost children or other loved ones in death, and some are just reporting public interest stories in the media. We want everyone we meet to know that even though the hurt never goes away, we are okay because God is faithful. We trust Him to provide for us. It is important that Dan's sacrifice is not forgotten. We, the Gold Star Family members, are the voices of our dead sons. If we don't tell their stories, the stories will not be told. This is the story of our son, a guy who chose to be happy and made every place he was a happier place to be. While a part of each one who knew Dan died with him, his memory continues to inspire every life he touched.

Made in the USA
Lexington, KY
28 May 2018